Idiots Are Everywhere
By Mike and Matt

Are you

What people are saying about the book!

"Excitingly funny! Both funny and exciting!!!" ~ Bill - an absolute no one

"Best read you'll ever have. Guaranteed!" ~ Tony - a man with no guaranteeing authority

"You'll laugh your socks off!" ~ Bill - once again, but this time wearing a fake mustache

"Buy it, you won't regret it! Actually, buy several copies. As many as you can." ~ The guys that wrote it

"The book is much better than the movie" ~ Anyone who reads books, but in this case there is no movie

Are you

Chapter Index

Are you

Disclaimer

The people referenced in this book are real, or maybe they're not. The situations are real, except in cases where they are not real. The names have been changed to protect the innocent…and the guilty.

If a name in the text matches yours, or someone you know, chances are, it's not you, or that person. Remember, there other people out there that share your first name.

If you think you are the only Dave, Steve, or Mary in the world, then you are an Idiot…

Are you

I

Join us as we talk to Idiots...

It's a world full of Idiots. Oh yes it is. Every single person reading this is thinking the exact same thing. "How...what...and why"... How is it possible that they're human, just like me? What exactly are they doing? Why are these people sharing the Earth with me? Do they not know they're Idiots? If they don't know, why is it that no one tells them? Every time you go somewhere...every time you do something...every time you try and have a normal moment in your life, you're surrounded by Idiots. Idiots are everywhere. If it wasn't for you, the whole planet would be nothing but Idiots. And maybe...just maybe...you're one too, and you're just not smart enough to figure it out. Or everyone you encounter is too much of an Idiot to tell you.

The formal (and now archaic and offensive) definition of an Idiot – A person of the lowest order, having a mental age of less than three and an IQ of under twenty-five.

There's an informal definition too – An utterly foolish or senseless person.

I sort of like the informal definition better, but come on. We all know what an Idiot is. In fact, someone taking the time to actually write out a specific definition is somewhat Idiotic, but I digress. The point is we've all seen Idiots. You've encountered Idiots. You've had dealings with Idiots.

More than likely, you're an Idiot too, so take heed. We're taking an in-depth and super-scientific look into Idiots. Idiots in public, Idiots in private. Where do they congregate? What do they do for fun? We're entering the real world and our mission is to expose Idiots. Hopefully to make it easier for the normal folk who are forced to encounter them in all their glory.

Think to yourself of all the instances where you've encountered an Idiot. You've probably wanted to ask them why. "Why are you, the way you are? Why did you just do that? That makes no sense, why are you saying that? Why are you acting like that? Don't you know it's ridiculous to wear that? Everything you're doing is wrong...why are you doing it?" The fact that every country has a word for Idiot pretty much proves they are everywhere. Call them Jabronis, call them Morons, call them Imbeciles, it makes no difference. They're everywhere.

Have you ever gone grocery shopping? Worked out in a gym? Frequented a public restroom? Ever been to a store? Ever had anything to eat? Yeah, us too, and we've got it covered. We've all seen them. We've all been there. We've all wanted to ask these Idiots just what the hell is "up." You can sit back and relax...we've done all the asking for you...

II

Everyone who drives is an Idiot...

Well, everyone else is, right? To devote a section in this book on Idiots who drive is a bit shortsighted. In reality we could do an entire book on that subject alone. But keeping things simple, let's just identify how many of you become bigger Idiots than you already are just by getting behind the wheel of a car.

Fact: Over 200 million people in the United States drive.
Idiot Fact: Over 198 million of them shouldn't.

Since everyone drives, it's really easy to find some people willing to give their two cents on the subject. And our range covers the entire country. Well, everything except Alaska and Hawaii. By the way, how Idiotic is it to have forty-eight states that are all connected and then have two off to the side? That would be like having an apartment with a living room, bedroom, and bathroom...then having the kitchen two blocks down. Couldn't we trade with Canada? Alaska for Quebec? Makes sense to me.

What about Idiotic bumper stickers? I don't care that you're proud of your honor roll student. If the kid got a B+ average would you disown him? Does he not deserve a sticker on the bumper that brings down the car value? Worse than that is the "My kid beat up your honor roll student" bumper sticker. That makes you and your thug kid Idiots.

The other day I got behind a construction vehicle and there was a warning sign plastered on the back that said "Do Not Follow Vehicle." Um…okay…can someone tell him not to go in the same direction as me then? Do I need to put a sticker on the front of my car that says "Don't drive in front of me?" Who wins in that case?

Anyway, we've talked to some drivers about Idiots on the road.

"Why the hell would you pass me on a one lane street then slam on your brakes as soon as you get in front of me to turn into a driveway? You couldn't just wait half a second? You numskull." ~ David- a part-time fisherman from Sioux Falls, SD.

"Some people drive just too damned slow. I pass em' just to learn em' some things. It's called teachin' em' basics." ~ Billy a slang talker – Sioux Falls, SD.

Here's a driving lesson for those of you that like to lay on the horn – don't lay on the horn. If the light goes green and you are blasting your horn one-tenth of a second later, you are an Idiot.

"Red lights are the worst damned things in the world. Worse than war. Worse than hunger. I friggin hate them!" ~ Impatient Ivan – Minneapolis, MN.

And people on motorcycles can be just as Idiotic. I love how they use hand signals for turning and passing, as if anyone outside of a sixteen year old who just took the road test knows what the hell the motorcyclist is doing. Is that guy on the bike stretching? Oh crap, I guess he's cutting me off. And how obnoxious is it when one guy on a motorcycle passes another and they do that silly wave to each other, like they're part of some secret fraternity of bike riders that we car people aren't cool enough to be included in. I think I'll start my own club. It's called "I can drive when it's raining or snowing and you can't, suck on that!"

"I wave at my fellow bikers. They wave back. It's cool and so am I. Don't be jealous. I didn't make the football team in high school, but no one can stop me from owning a bike!" ~ Henry "Hog Wild" Harrison – Mobile, AL.

And why is it I could be driving a two-ton Hummer with bulletproof doors, windshield and pillow soft airbags surrounding me, and still get a ticket if my seatbelt isn't on, but some guy can race down the street at a hundred miles an hour on the back of a bike with no protection whatsoever as long as he's wearing a helmet? A helmet is not going to do anything to help if he flies off anyway.

"I ride my bike. I love the feeling of the wind and the fresh air from behind my helmet. And I can hear the beautiful sounds of nature drown out from the roar and diesel of my engine." ~ Gunther T – Tallahassee, FL.

One of the worst things about driving is getting pulled over. We've all been there. Seeing those red lights flashing is a terrifying feeling. By the way, do you think cops get nervous when I pull out of a parking lot and speed up behind one of them? Probably not, why would they? That was a pretty dumb comparison by me.

Anyway, the lights go on, sometimes you even hear a siren. Your first thought is that you committed the worst crime in the history of crimes. Butterflies immediately start racing in your stomach. Speeding? Running a stop light? Driving on two wheels? I once got pulled over because my tint was too dark on my windows. I offered the name of the shop that did the tinting, since it's apparently illegal. He gave me the ticket instead. Oh crap, there's my cell phone on the passenger seat! Did he think I was texting? I wasn't texting. Only Idiots would text and drive. It's his word against mine, what if he says I was texting? What if one of my Idiot friend's texts me while he's at the window? Oh the horror!

Sometimes you get a reprieve. He's not after you at all; it's someone else he wants. I'm innocent I tell ya, innocent! Maybe some bandits are robbing a stagecoach just ahead of me. Maybe a brawl broke out at the old saloon. Hopefully he is going to shoot past me at high speeds to catch the real criminal – a swashbuckling blacksmith who stole some spices and tea.

You pull over. The cop doesn't drive past you…he's pulling over too. Great! So you sit and wait and the door behind you slowly opens. A female officer, who looks nothing like the cops on TV, starts walking up. You prepare for a barrage of stupid questions.

Where were you going?

Let's see. I'm in a shirt and tie. It's seven-thirty on a Wednesday morning. There's a large business park a mile ahead and there is a briefcase on the seat. I'm going to Disney World!

Do you know what speed zone you are in?

Speed zone…is that some new deodorant? Besides, a speed zone actually sounds fast. Why don't you cut to the chase?

Do you know how fast you were going?

And there it is. Honestly I don't, but I'm not going to say that. The speed limit is forty-five. Obviously I was going over that or I wouldn't be idling on the shoulder of the road right now. I fudge the number a bit, let's say…fifty…

You were going fifty-four.

Then why did you ask if you already knew the answer? I guess it was rhetorical? Irrelevant since either way you were speeding.

License and registration…

Now of course I have to start digging for my paperwork, seeing as I never have to use it. Does anyone know where it is? I start pulling random papers out of my glove compartment like a clown pulling handkerchiefs from his mouth. Seems like my glove compartment contains every piece of junk I have ever had that doesn't fit in the center console. Ironically my gloves are stuffed into the side compartment of my door. Okay let's see…my student ID from four years ago…a useless calendar my insurance agent sent as a Christmas gift…there's the receipt from the camera I wanted to return…oooh! Gum!

After what seems like an hour of fumbling around in the glove box, I finally find it. The cop takes it back to her car. I sit and wait as she runs my plates to see if I'm a speeder…or something worse. Sure I'm a speeder, but is that all? Did I take care of that registration tag on time? I once skipped swim class in junior high school - is there some long overdue outstanding warrant to haul me in? That's how they get all those crooks on 'COPS' or 'America's Most Wanted.' It starts with a routine traffic stop and then they get nailed for being a serial killer. Wait, have I killed anyone? Do I floss enough?

And now of course every Idiot driving passed me has to slow down and stare. "Keep driving pal. No I didn't rob a bank and no, you don't know me." Finally, the officer comes back and presents me with a ticket. She talks really fast. All I catch is 'plead guilty,' 'slow it down,' and 'have a great day.'

Have a great day? Is that possible now? How much is this going to cost? Am I getting points on my license? Do I now have to take a ten-hour course? What about that guy that just drove by, he must have been speeding too…go get him!

I start reading the options on the ticket. Do I need a fancy lawyer? He can probably get the ticket reduced or even dropped. Of course his fees will cost twice what the ticket would. If I go to court, will the judge wear a white powdered wig? Do I get to yell: "You can't handle the truth?"

Since this has happened before to everyone I talk to, I know the routine. The judge will ask if I was speeding. I will say no. The ticket will get reduced and I will pay a fine. In fact, for my convenience of course, I can just plead by mail and not waste any time at all. I can just send them the check or my debit card number. It is so nice of them to make it more convenient for me to give them my money. Thanks!

Aren't traffic violations strange? I get pulled over for speeding. I plead not guilty. The judge reduces it to running a stop sign. I agree. End of case. Where else in a courtroom would that logic work? I robbed a bank. I plead not guilty. The judge reduces it to insurance fraud. I say okay. So basically, in a place where you aren't supposed to lie in front of a judge, it is the judge that ends up lying.

Have you ever been pulled over on a trip? Here I am, two-hundred miles from home and now there is no chance at all of not getting a ticket because this small town cop knows I'm not going to drive all the way back here just to plead not guilty in court. And why is court never like it is on TV? No lawyers, no expert witnesses. It takes five seconds and I always lose no matter what. One time I got a ticket reduced to some random non-moving violation. The cost of the fine was $60. That wasn't bad. The cost of the court fee was $70. So the total of the reduced ticket was $130. Come on.

And don't you love lawyers that advertise that they specialize in getting you off of DUI charges? Great. You're doing your community a great service. Drink up people, we have lawyers standing by! Call our toll free number! Burn down twenty houses? No problem! Call Attorney Johnny Sleazeball now! Our firm specializes in defending arsonists too! Forget that pesky jail room...we'll have you back on the streets by lunch!

And why do lawyers have to come up with their own language to confuse the hell out of you and in the end have the upper hand. They want the security to know you don't know what the heck you are signing and have to rely on them to translate. That isn't fair! Why can't it be written in English?

And why is it that every driver thinks it's okay to go five miles an hour over the speed limit? That's great logic. Yup, just set the cruise to speeding and be on your way. The assumption is that police don't mind as long as it's within five miles of the speed limit. So if I see a pair of sneakers that I like, and the price tag says $65, does the store expect $70? Can I get away with only paying $60?

And here's a novel concept; if you are driving, JUST DRIVE! Some Idiots think that they can catch up on everything else in life they have to do while driving. Forget to write a book report? No problem, I have a forty-five minute commute to the school. Need to do your makeup? No worries! Just hit the snooze and apply on the way to work. Hell, I once saw a guy shaving his face with an electric razor as he drove by me. Need to eat but can't wait five minutes? Need to respond to a friend's text message about a Seinfeld rerun?

People tend to do whatever it takes to put everyone else in danger. You're only driving a two-thousand pound assault weapon that is barreling down the road at high speeds. And for goodness sake…hang up the damn phone. I don't understand the people that grab the phone and start dialing the second they get into the car. You couldn't have called before getting in? Trust me; you're not that important that whatever call you have to make can't wait until you're home.

"I was addicted to a reality TV show. I didn't have time to watch it last night, but I got a really boring commute. It's only driving right? And I do the drive every day. I could practically do it with my eyes closed! The episode was great but I ended up stuck in a corn field. That part wasn't so great." ~ Alex - sock salesman – Lincoln, NE.

III

Working with Idiots

Fact: There are about 152.7 million employed in the U.S.
Idiot Fact: .7 of them actually work while at their job.

It's seven o'clock in the morning and "Cat Scratch Fever" starts blasting from my radio. What Idiot disc jockey thought playing this song this early was a good idea? Hell, why is he even playing it at all? I guess it's my fault since I chose the soothing sounds of music over the cacophonous blasting beeping alarm tone. But how can I be asked to start my day with "Cat Scratch Fever?" How can I handle work, or anything for that matter, with that song now permanently etched in my brain? Is it now stuck in your head? Sorry. I'd rather start the day with someone dumping a bucket of ice cold water on my face.

As I walk into my freezing cold bathroom to take a shower, I begin to wonder to myself as I do every morning…why is the bathroom always so cold? You could have the heat blasting in the house, but the bathroom will always feel like a walk-in cooler. Perfect really, since it is the only room in the house where I'm consistently naked and soaking wet.

"Let's make it the coldest room in the house!" ~ John Bathroom, the obvious inventor of the bathroom.

And not only is it the coldest room, it contains the coldest single element as well – the toilet. Great! Now your non-calloused and super sensitive butt cheeks can sit on a block of ice first thing in the morning, like some nut ice fishing in Saskatchewan. James Toilet is just as much of a jerk as John Bathroom.

And why is it so loud in there? Every sound you make is amplified louder than a Led Zeppelin concert. I'm trying to be quiet because people are sleeping and I drop my razor. It sounds like I just dropped a bowling ball. And forget about being discrete while going to the bathroom, it sounds like you're playing a trumpet or tuba in the marching band. No one is going to believe there is a marching band in the bathroom, nobody!

After my Alaskan shower, I make some breakfast, pack a lunch like a second-grader, and it's off to the office. Now I know why some people buy lunch. Making a sandwich in the morning is torturous. But since the cafeteria at work charges one-million dollars for a turkey wrap that has more lettuce than turkey, I'll stick with bringing my own.

Before dealing with the Idiots most people encounter at work, coffee is in order. McDonald's is on the way so I reluctantly stop there. They only charge $1 for a large coffee. I love the taste of their coffee, but should I be suspicious? I also like all of their food, but rumor has it that it's made out of something other than what you think it is. So I guess it's my own fault for thinking it would be good for you. Can they actually make coffee bad for you? Knowing McDonald's, I wouldn't doubt it if they deep fried it first, but it sure does taste good.

The kid taking my order asks how many "milks" I want in the coffee. I know the United States is the only country in the world that doesn't use the metric system, but I don't recall ever learning about "milks" as a unit of measure. And why do they even ask since no matter what I say they are going to put whatever they feel like in it anyway. After confirming twice that I don't want to try the Breakfast McRib or add an Apple Pie, I'm off to the first of many windows.

The first window represents the pay-up window. Of course we all know one dollar really means one-dollar-and-eight-cents. I have cash but really don't want a handful of change so I hand over my debit card. Even though it's just a cup of coffee, they still hand me a receipt the size of small flag as though I'm going to return it someday. Maybe I can present it to the Emergency Room as proof for why I'm no doubt going to visit there.

The next window is the food window. Although I only ordered a large coffee, oftentimes I am handed a bag of food by mistake. Being the keen individual that I am, I know right away that a Styrofoam cup looks nothing like a greasy sack of food. After explaining to the Idiot at the window that I didn't order a breakfast of 8,000 calories, I am finally on my way to work.

As I pull into the parking lot at work, of course all the good spots are taken. I drive twenty miles or so through the lot, past the front doors, and park at the very end. Then I walk the twenty miles back through the lot to the doors. Then it's through the giant lobby, complete with motivational posters that make no sense and large portraits of smiling employees that are all too happy and good looking to actual be working here. I climb the steps and walk to my desk, which is of course the furthest one away from the entrance to the room. It took ten minutes to drive here from home, and it's now been twelve minutes since I got out of my car. And nothing is worse than arriving a few minutes late while clutching a giant coffee. You're basically flaunting that you could have been on time but decided to stop off for a drink first.

"Don't talk to me until I've had my coffee!" ~ Margaret - a miserable co-worker who you didn't want to talk to anyway, because regardless of whether or not she has had coffee, she's still an asshole.

Everyone works with Idiots. All co-workers, all managers, everyone. Everyday I'm thinking to myself – where the hell did this company find these people? They are, after all, completely un-hirable elsewhere. A break room debate was raging the other day between two hefty women over which color M&M was their favorite. As if there is a difference, especially when they're stuffing dozens at a time down their throats, with those catchers' mitts they call hands.

And if I hear one more person come back from vacation and say that they are glad to be back because they were bored, I'm really going to lose it. Seriously? You were bored and thought a better option for fun is to be here? You couldn't take a walk? Read a book? Watch TV? Sleep in? Wouldn't any of those things be better than work? "I like my routine." He says. Idiot! I prefer my freedom.

So I reach my desk and now it's time to fire up the 'ole' computer. I begin to notice that my work passwords are often times more challenging and complicated than the work I'm doing itself. Let's see, counting my login, my work queue, human resources…five carry the one…I only need four-billion different passwords to get through my day. And of course, managers tell you not to write them down. If you do, the bad guys may find them and be able to access some meaningless reports, and I guess, see how boring my job actually is. Sure, I won't write them down. I'll just commit to memory a twelve character password that has exactly one number, one special character, no more than three but no less than one uppercase letter, and needs to be changed every sixty days but can't be at all similar to anything I've ever used before. And they wonder why I need so many breaks. Stress, anxiety, eyestrain, migraines…and that's all just trying to get the damned computer on.

And every time I call, I always think that they have special equipment showing them what my secret password is, which is really embarrassing since my current password is CuddlyBear@5. And please don't ask for my security questions.

And don't enter the wrong password. If you do, the system kindly locks you out like a chastity belt, forcing you to call the ominous 'Help Desk' or, as the older women that sit near me refer to it, the "Helpless Desk." And of course how dumb do you feel if you can't remember your own password? The Help Desk guys that take these calls minored in computers and majored in social ineptitude. They often work from home, usually their parents basement, and enjoy helping people about as much as I enjoy having to memorize four billion passwords that are twelve characters long containing exactly one number, one special character, no more than three but no less than one uppercase letter, and needs to be changed every sixty days but can't be at all similar to anything I've ever used before etc., etc.

When I finally get the stupid computer on, the first thing I do is check my email. The usual suspects are here; junk from some corporate big-wig, someone talking about Friday Happy Hour already on Monday morning, and of course, six or seven messages from six or seven Idiots that hit the infamous "reply to all" button on the corporate execs message. And it's never enough that one Idiot did it. Now a handful of Idiots keep doing it and that's what drives me up the wall. Read the buttons before you send! Otherwise all twenty-seven-thousand of us are getting your stupid message! Then there is the type of person who replies all with something completely useless on purpose to show you that he is a participator. "Sounds good." Great, thanks for your reply Idiot!

Accompanying emails for annoyance is the dreaded Instant Messenger. Most offices employ some form of Instant Messenger as a way to quickly communicate with employees. Workers can enter group chats with co-workers so if they run into an issue, they can post questions in real time to get an answer or assistance.

Of course, the ability to type a message to someone across the aisle or across the ocean wasn't enough. Some Idiot had to develop the Emoticon. So not only can I get an answer to my question I can see exactly how you feel!

That was a good question! ☺ - Like seriously, you can't always be happy.

Good point! ;) ;) – Don't wink at me.

I don't know the answer :\ - I assumed you wouldn't, you're a dumbass.

That makes me sad. ☹ - Really? *That* makes you sad? Wow, I hope I'm never around you if something serious actually happens.

And every office has that one person who has a billion different Emoticons stored away for use with every occasion. They went to cornyemoticons.com and stocked up.

It's Midges birthday. Happy birthday Midge! That's not enough. I need a stupid bouncing yellow smiley face diving like a hog into a cake.

TGIF! Not enough. I need to be treated to an intoxicated cartoon ball guzzling booze from a barrel.

This job sucks! Accompanied with an Emoticon jumping off of a cliff.

My computer is messing up. Oh, this is a good one, an Emoticon senselessly beating a monitor with a bat.

The list goes on. A dancing penguin, a silly bear, a crude Santa for Christmas etc… Apparently this is how we display emotion in today's technological cyber world. Our feelings now elevated to the next level.

So I've been here for an hour. I've finally gotten through the password barricades and muddled through two dozen senseless emails. By the way do these people ever sleep? I left at six o'clock and the email box was empty. How is it full again at eight the next morning? We've logged into the group chat and said good morning to every single person and encountered several new Emoticons to boot such as an obnoxious grinning sun wearing spectacles and what appears to be an ostrich drinking. Time to get to work right? NOPE! Time for a meeting!!! I'm sure the stockholders and customers would approve. ;)

Meetings

Fact: 11 million meetings are held per day in the U.S.
Idiot Fact: 10,999,952 of them accomplish nothing.

Meetings are a great way to waste time, especially if
you're someone who is less than important. Meetings consist
of many different people chiming in at random times for no
other reason than to hear themselves talk. Meetings seldom, if
ever, accomplish anything. The next time you sit through a
meeting, ask yourself after if it was a good and productive use
of time. Chances are it wasn't. I usually start off paying
attention, but by the time the introduction is over, my eyes are
wandering around to the other people in the room. I like to
play games like "What's up with that moron?" or "What
idiotic idea does she have today?" and before I know it, we're
adjourning.

So we all enter one of the fifty conference rooms, and
everyone has to comment on how much more comfortable the
chairs are in here. You need to quickly decipher if it's going to
be a good meeting, or a bad meeting. Signs of a good meeting:
balloons, cake and smiling managers. Signs of a bad meeting
usually involve frowning faces in designer suits, strangers
from underdeveloped cheaper waged countries, or the HR
guy lurking around in the shadows. Posters or slides
depicting cost-cutting or ways to make things "better" for the
customer are never a good sign either. Since the CEO isn't
reducing his seven-figure salary, or giving back any of that
bonus he got last quarter, the only way to benefit the
customer's usually involves the employees getting laid off.

One way is outsourcing (or 'sourcing' as they cleverly put it to try and fool you). The Idiot execs explain that due to low stock prices, fifty of us are being replaced with one-hundred people from Calcutta. But don't worry; this will help us in the long run as our pension will be fully vested when we retire. Great! What good is money going to do me when I'm seventy, if I starve to death at thirty-five? Everyone in the room is somber. How to liven things up? How about a motivational quote from Gandhi! How cute. By the way, didn't he starve to death too?

Thankfully, all signs point to a good meeting. Meaning I can relax, look at other people, and wonder just why the hell I'm in here. Sometimes they recognize my co-workers with a balloon and a thunderous round of applause. No thanks, if I do something good you can just cut me a check. One good meeting was to go over the CEO's vision, which was for the company to be the most admired and exceptional one there is. Gee, really? Is that what he wants? We need a meeting for this?

Have you noticed that every meeting has Mister or Misses Noisemaker? These are the Idiots who can't attend meetings without props. Coffee cups to slurp from, cough drop wrappers to crunch and crumble, water bottles to squeeze, salads to munch on…the list goes on and on. Do you really need an extra-large water bottle? Are you that thirsty?

Want to make the meeting even more wasteful? Try ordering food for everyone. Great idea if your meeting agenda is making a mess and getting nothing accomplished. It's impossible to chew in silence for most people, and no one can talk and eat at the same time. At least, they shouldn't. People are tearing into pizza. Diet Cokes are tossed around like footballs. The people that think they're healthy are busy licking the lids of their yogurt containers. And no one is paying attention to our fearless leader, stammering on about company morale, more profits and customer excellence. Here's an idea to boost morale…I would rather be eating at a restaurant with people I actually like!

The only thing worse is a meeting at a bar. Good luck trying to get your silly point across to people buzzed from beer. This is usually an execs way of showing he is "one of us." Just a commoner, throwing back a bottle of hops and munching on chicken wings with us working stiffs. Really? One of us? This is the same guy that arrived from the corporate office this morning on a gold plated helicopter flanked by five assistants and a small security detail. Oh but wait…he's a Bud Light drinker! He's just like me! Let's have two pal! Even though if you notice closely, he won't even finish one.

Participation in meetings shows you're on top of things at work. Or does it? Everyone knows the same people that ask questions during every meeting, and their usually the company brown-nosers. They make key points such as, "If we really bear down and work hard on this project, we can get a lot done in a short time." Uh…really? Go figure. I always thought if we were slow and lazy it would get done faster. Good thing you're here professor! Where would we be without you?

And what Idiot came up with the expression, "There are no stupid questions." You obviously haven't attended any of my meetings. The CEO comes in from headquarters to announce massive layoffs and there's Bridget raising her hand to ask if we can still wear sneakers on Friday. Yes sweetie, you'll need to be comfortable in the unemployment line.

And is the meeting ever really over? Have you ever had a meeting about a meeting? After sitting for an hour discussing nonsense, you then find yourself scheduling another meeting to talk about something you either forgot to cover or didn't cover enough. Last week I had a "quick" meeting to discuss an upcoming meeting next week. Great, that should occupy my entire afternoon, I can't wait! My future looks bright!

Managers

**Fact: 70% of management positions make more than $50k per year.
Idiot Fact: Most employees think they know more than their
manager.**

What would the workforce do without our managers?
Behind the outside toughness of every manager is a wimpy
soul. Sure they seem to have things together, but in reality
they are just the same as you, elevated one pay grade and
dealing with a lot more crap. And they are like that in every
work environment there is. I used to work at a grocery store
and had a manager that would begin every command with the
words "If you want." He would say something like, "If you
want, you can start unloading the truck." As if I would ever
want to do that. "If you want, you can start working on those
California file reports." Hmmm....let me see.....nah....I think
what I want is to go back to my nice warm bed. Thanks
anyway though.

One time recently the power went out in my office. My
manager decided the way to get through this very difficult
time, was to remind us to "stay busy." This is a rather
interesting approach seeing as our entire job is done over the
computer. Now, how exactly should I stay busy? Maybe I can
just move some papers around. File some stuff? Oh wait, we
are now completely paperless. How about if I pull out a
vacuum and start cleaning up? Oh wait, the power is out, that
won't work either. The guy outside with the riding mower
looks like he is having much more fun than I am. Maybe I
should see if he needs any help.

And why is it that whenever any manager is giving an example, they always use the name Suzie? If Suzie calls in, this happens. Suzie was late to work. Suzie didn't do her report on time. If I were the manager, I'd fire this Suzie person immediately.

I once had a manager bragging that they were a Six-Sigma black belt. Six Sigma is a set of strategies, techniques, and tools for process improvement. It doesn't mean he can fight in the UFC... It means he spent a lot of company time, money and resources, studying how to save the company time, money and resources. Hmmm...I have a better way to do that, and my belt is an adjustable piece of crap from Kohl's.

Team Building

Fact: The goal of team building is to support each other.
Idiot Fact: Most team members would rather not support each other.

Anyway, it's now time to read a follow-up email to this morning's meeting. I open an email and it's got a summary. Evidently our production is starting to dwindle a little, and to make sure we stay on top of things, the most logical next step is in order: A team building exercise! We're going to put people together from different departments who don't know each other and force them to interact. That should turn morale around right?

So rather than leaving us alone, we're going to put Carlos from IT and Joanne from Accounting together for a three-legged race. The Director of Social Media would be ecstatic to go on a scavenger hunt with Tina from the Art Department, who hasn't said two words since she was hired. Ben from the Mailroom is stoked for a water balloon toss with Kendra the receptionist. They both have great ideas for taking us to the next level (though Ben's wife may not be too pleased with the pairing).

What's great is that these events are designed for employees to have fun, but there is not one single employee who likes doing them. Management should try actually *thinking* about what would be fun before coming up with this crap. Idiots!

"My pits start sweating every time I hear the words...team building exercise." ~ Gargamel - Casper, WY.

"I hate that lady in accounting. She is a pain in the you know what. Can I swear? Anyway, all she does is chase down money and harp on people for not paying on time. She's miserable. Can I name names? It's Thelma. I don't want nothing to do with that hag." ~ Bobby – Rutland, VT.

"I don't want to even talk to these people let alone run an obstacle course with them. I'd rather just sit with my headphones on and do some work." ~ Pepe – Milton, DE.

"Oh I think it's absolutely great! I think it will really help Gladys break out of her shell and become more social. We'll learn great new techniques that we can use for years to come." ~ Michelle – Coral Springs, FL.

"Michelle is an Idiot. I hate her, she sucks on all levels. If only she knew everyone hates her." ~ Gladys – Coral Springs, FL.

"No one is touching Secret Santa. I do it every year and it's mine. Everyone likes it and they like that I do it." ~ Faith – Peoria, IL.

"As a manager who considers himself a hands-on manager, I enjoy organizing team building exercises for my staff. The troops as I like to call them. They like that. I usually title the memo something clever like, 'Wanna have some fun?' because I think if I tell them it's fun, they will be onboard." ~ George – Utica, NY.

Lunchtime

**Fact: 60% of workers work through their lunch break
Idiot Fact: The other 40% are smart.**

It's almost lunch time so I go to use the rest room and wash my hands. Of course I have to wait because the giant yellow janitor cart is blocking the door along with a "Do not enter" sign that looks like it was stolen from an episode of CSI. Why is it they have to clean the bathrooms at noon when everyone is going to lunch? Wouldn't it make more sense to do it at… say, eleven a.m.? Or, how about midnight? That would be even better. And I love it when they spend twenty minutes cleaning and then I go in only to find no paper towels, or the soap empty from one of the sinks. What the hell were they doing the whole time they were in there?

So now you've been at work for several hours, and not one damn thing has been accomplished. It's time for lunch!

Lunch can be a tricky thing when you're at work and you're dealing with Idiots. Sometimes you bring your own lunch, avoiding the inflated prices of the cafeteria and the peer pressure of going to Chipotle. The problem with bringing your own lunch to work is there is nowhere to escape to eat it. The cafeteria is packed. The breakroom is full of buffoons. People are always using conference rooms. There's a table outside but some Idiot spider is already there. What to do?

You choose the breakroom since there is no way of avoiding people. You sit down and brace yourself for the barrage of stupid questions, such as, "What you got there? Spaghetti? Spaghetti on a Tuesday? Did you make it yourself? How do you do your sauce? You can cook?"

The small fraction of time that belongs to me has just become an episode of Dateline. I'm half expecting that creepy guy from "To Catch a Predator" to walk in surrounded with cameras. "Yes people, its spaghetti!" I thought for certain the long string like macaroni would have given it away.

Why are you so shocked that I can cook? I'm a grown man. It's not that hard to boil water and empty a box into it. And the sauce? I hope you're sitting down for this – open a can and pour it in. Presto-magico. You should try it yourself Sherlock.

"As a boss, I like to stroll into the lunchroom to see what the troops are talking about. I like to keep them on their toes and let them know they are still at work and not some swanky pub with their friends. I usually hover over them like a vulture and ask what they are eating. I am pretty sure everyone likes it when I do that. I'm a cool manager, but I also keep them sharp." ~ Gary - a random manager.

There's also the option of ordering in, but then of course this is more complicated than your work, your passwords, and your meeting about the meeting. No one ever wants to call. "What if someone hears me talking?" I doubt they will care, people talk all the time. Looks like I'm stuck setting everything up again. "Can I substitute the fries for a salad?" I don't know, I don't work there remember? I wish I did, and then I wouldn't be stuck with you.

Collecting the money is nearly impossible. "How much do I owe?" Let's see. Your burger was $6. So with tax and tip, I'd say a little more than that. I'm not your accountant. By the way, don't you work in accounting? And no I can't break a hundred; I'm not your banker either. The only people worse are the cheapskates that figure it out to the penny. "You owe me twenty-six cents. I prefer an American quarter and a 1970s Indonesian penny, if you have it." I don't. In fact, next time I prefer you don't order.

The order arrives and there is always one thing wrong. "Hey! My tuna sandwich has whipped cream on it!" Sucks to be you pal. Next time *you* place the order. And of course there's the one Idiot who gets upset that they weren't included. "Gee, thanks for inviting me. Just kidding, just kidding." Listen you passive aggressive jackass, I've sat near you for two years and we've never spoken. Next time I'll ask all five-hundred people on the floor if they want in. Or how about you just order your own?

The next option is going out for lunch. You'd think this would translate to peace and quiet away from the office. A select couple of friends can get together and complain about work. But like bloodhounds, people you don't like get wind of the scheme and suddenly they are coming along too. And of course there's Luke who no one likes but he sits at the desk in the front of the room. It's impossible to sneak by him without him seeing. So he's now invited also. Great. Lunch just turned into an awful hour. Maybe tomorrow I should just hide under my desk.

Sometimes we'll even do a "food day" at work where everyone just brings in a different dish to pass around. This is always an excuse to overeat and accomplish nothing. Usually everyone complains that they are too busy and don't want to participate. Then they see how great another team's "food day" looks and everyone gets jealous. And I love how several women find it necessary to mention, as they are loading their plates like a feeding trough, how they won't be having dinner that night because they are eating so much now.

A) I don't care.

B) Sure you're not.

"I hate it when my coworkers don't ask me to lunch even though I never talk to them. They should at least be polite and ask me. I usually make a comment like 'thanks for inviting me.' That usually shows them it doesn't bother me." ~ Monica – Dayton, OH.

"I eat at my desk which suits me to a tee. But how come the lady that sits next to me has to mention that I got sunburn over the weekend? Like did she think I didn't notice or something? Or like when she always comments to me about the weather. Like she'll tell me it's really cold out. Like I didn't notice when I was out there. Thanks for the update, Captain Obvious." ~ Shawn – an antisocial desk clerk.

Office Celebrations

How awkward is it when someone in the company that you don't know, or have never even seen, retires? Normally it wouldn't matter if a complete stranger decides to ride off into the sunset, but of course, some Idiot decides a card and collection is in order. Now I have to scrounge up a couple of dollars for a guy I've never even spoken to. Then the card gets passed around. Someone signs it and drops it off at my desk while I'm at the printer. I come back and have no idea what to say to this guy. I start reading what the other people wrote and decide to plagiarize from a combination of what three other people said.

"Dear Hank, it was great working with you, even though we didn't work together. Congrats and good luck with everything, even if I have no idea what you are going to do. Enjoy the money I threw in, because I surely won't."

I always write 'Congrats,' because I am nervous I will spell congratulations wrong under this pressure situation. Once it's signed, I'm now stuck having to figure out who gets it next. I walk over to the woman in front of me but she sees the card and quickly waves me off, as if I am walking over with a live python. No no, she informs me, I already signed it. Great! Now I have to come up with a plan and sneak around like a cat burglar to make sure Hank doesn't see the card. I will drop it off on Bob's desk the next time he goes to the printer. Then I will slither away on the floor like the Grinch, thus pawning off the responsibility.

I've signed more cards for strangers at work then my own family. And it's not just retirements; you have weddings, birthdays and baby showers. It might be easier to just have my check direct deposited into a special occasions account.

"Anytime there is a celebration to be had, I am on it. I go right up to people and demand money from them. It feels great to give back. I don't care if people know the person I am collecting for, it makes me feel good and that's all that matters. Plus the person always knows I organize it, because I make it a point to tell them." ~ Veronica - office celebration organizer

"It is nice to get a card and some cash for my retirement party. To be frankly honest though, it is very awkward for me to take it and I put the card in the trashcan right away. I don't even read the messages." ~ Carl – Retiree

IV

Idiots must eat too

Fact: 100% of the population eats
Idiot Fact: I had to look that stat up

It's Friday night and after dealing with Idiots all week, it's time for some weekend fun. Friday night means dinner with friends. Great food, some drinks, and laughs abound. Oh waiter, more wine please! Is there any way a great time won't be had?

Yes. Idiots can end up joining you as well.

Friends are great but sometimes they can make dinner stressful by introducing wildcards.

"Is it okay if I bring my friends to dinner? They're really cool guys. They love to eat food and drink liquid, just like us. You will love them. They like the Yankees." – Friends who hype up friends because they know everyone won't like them.

Oh well then. By all means bring them along. I mean come on. They like to eat and drink. And Yankees fans to boot? I mean no one is a Yankees fan so that must mean I will love them.

Don't you cringe when you show up only to find out that they have been drinking? They order several thousand expensive mixed drinks before anyone else gets there. A

Passion Colada, a Beach Iced Tea (a clever variation of the Long Island Iced Tea). Next it's the Blue Lagoon. The bill is now at fifty dollars and they haven't cracked a buzz.

Normally this wouldn't matter. Except of course when the waiter (who is really a professional musician, but works as a waiter) suggests combining all the checks onto one bill. Thanks! Can you also let me pay their rent? Not only is this easier for the waiter, but it will also insure that I will get the ole' screw job in about two hours. And you always feel that you have to go along with this situation. If you ask for separate checks you look like the cheapskate with your friends and the waiter will scowl at you as though you just asked him to memorize Deuteronomy. You don't know what Deuteronomy is? Me either. I had to look it up after I read it.

"You want me to break up the bill? That is nearly impossible to do. You should have asked me two weeks ago. I don't nearly have enough time to figure out how to do that. I'm going to make some face and hand gestures now to make you feel guilty for asking me that question. Thanks for ruining my night!" – Every waiter

So you watch as the cosmos keep getting ordered and the tab keeps climbing. It's like you're sitting in the back of a cab, stuck in traffic while the meter is ticking away your life savings.

Then it gets worse.

It turns out someone at the table is a self-proclaimed wine aficionado. He attended a sampling once at the local zoo wine tasting event and read an article in Maxim, so be prepared to be blown away. In reality the only thing they know is that the highest priced bottle is probably the best so the Idiot points to that. "Ah yes my good man. We'll take a bottle of Chianti Broussard from 1827. Cheerio."

The wine is delivered and a nose goes into the bottle like a bloodhound searching for the scent of a pheasant. The only difference is the bloodhound knows what it's doing. "It's good! My nose can tell these things." Like anyone has ever said that wine is bad. So now we have confirmation that it's okay to drink and get to hear further useless knowledge about crushed grapes picked from a specific vine in some French town no one has ever heard of and a bottle sitting in a darkened cellar for a decade.

How can we start to make things at the dinner table awkward? The introduction of the bread basket, that's how. The bread basket has the ability to be one of, if not the single most awkward times in your life. Why can't the cooks just cut the bread all the way through? You reach in and grab a piece and it's clinging with fervor to another section of the loaf. Now my hands are all over the entire thing as I tear apart my section like some Viking in the galley of a ship. Ripping and tugging like a raccoon in a garbage can. I got it! Everyone I did it! I got a piece! Now what should I do? Should I create a diversion so I can sneak the crumpled remains of the other piece back in the basket? Does anyone have a rabbit I can pull out of a hat? But really, who wants to eat that? I've had my hands all over it and it now resembles a mangled piece of trash. Do the cooks cut it that way on purpose? Do they get tired out half way through the cutting process and think they can just pour olive oil on a plate to distract us from the uncut bread?

The only distraction and saving grace from the bread at this point is the appetizer menu. Grab that sucker and make some small talk about spinach dip. Most apps (what cool people call appetizers) are the size and cost of an entire meal and are completely unneeded but we live in America, so we have to stuff our faces. Here goes the bill again. Do people really need to eat crab filled lobster tails, caviar and truffles before dinner? Okay, who ordered a Rolex with a side of BMW?

How about the person who orders appetizers and pretends they didn't realize how big it would be. "Oh waiter, I am on a diet. I will take the Nacho's Supreme, but with no lettuce." She (or he) then acts all shocked when it arrives. "Wow!" She (or he) exclaims as she (or he) begins to dig in. "I didn't expect it to be so much food." Really? What did you think they meant by supreme?

Wow, this is getting fun. Is there anything else we can do after eating a loaf of bread and four plates of apps (again, cool word for appetizers and way easier to spell)? It's dinner time! The waiter starts running down the list of specials and I usually space out like I do during the meetings at work or just stare blankly at the menu and nod as if I care what he is saying. Like, if I came here intent on Prime Rib this bozo is going to make me change my mind to the Chilean Sea Bass.

There is always that one time where I hear a word I like though. "Today's specials are: blah blah blah blah blah blah chicken wings, blah blah." Woah woah woah wait a second. What was that chicken wings one again? "The dish is chicken wings cooked in capers and trout juice. " Oh, screw that. Those specials aren't so special pal! Let me go back to ignoring you. Sometimes I'll ask what they recommend as if the waiter could possibly know what food I like. Imagine walking up to a cashier at a grocery store and asking what they recommend. They give their advice and I immediately order something else making them feel like an Idiot. Or maybe that just makes me look like an Idiot? Hey wait a sec…

The meal is then delivered one plate at a time. The polite thing to do is to wait until everyone is served before eating. Of course, I'm sitting here with starving animals so they begin to pick at a fry or a carrot as if that is not really considered eating. I love that logic. It's only a fry… basically the same as not eating at all. Or they offer you something so they can start. "Would you like a bite of my soup?" As if you are going to take some. No, I don't want a bite of your soup.

Finally we are all eating and of course everyone has to ask how my food is, like I am a five year old. One Idiot has to send a steak back. They asked for it medium. It was not medium enough apparently. I've never once sent food back in my entire life. Remember, no matter how imperfect it may be, it's still much better than anything you could have made yourself. Some people just don't understand that it's never a good idea to insult the person preparing your food.

"Hey buddy, you clearly don't know what you are doing in your own profession. I wanted it cooked this way and you were so off that I have to send it back. Now if you could please get a brain, take my food back and fix it nicely for me, I would appreciate it. What a doll you are!" –Person who will be eating food that has been down the cook's pants.

When the meal is done, the waiter asks us if we've saved room for dessert, which is really a disgusting concept and a testament to why American's are so obese. After guzzling a dozen high caloric drinks, eating bread, appetizers, a salad and then a full meal...can your fat stomach handle a slice of cheese cake drizzled with strawberry syrup? Normal people say no but of course it goes from a couple people sharing dessert to everyone realizing they are paying for others eating it, to everyone ordering their own.

TGIF? How about TG Friday's Over.

"I love to drink as much alcohol as I can if I know we are splitting the bill. This way I make out pretty well. I also don't hesitate to add an extra meatball here and there. I know I'm not paying for it!" ~ Quincy – Flagstaff, AZ.

"Drinking wine makes me feel superior to my counterparts at dinner. I like to say the name of the wine in an accent when ordering. It makes me feel a bit more intelligent than the common beer or soda drinker." ~ Allison – Wilmington, DE.

When on your own, eating habits are different. If I want something simple, cheap, and tasty, I sometimes head to

Subway. Of course, Idiots have the same plan too. After standing in line for fifteen minutes, it was time for the guy in front of me to order. He of course had no clue what he wanted. Why couldn't he have decided in the fifteen minutes that we stood there? And if that wasn't bad enough, he acted as though it was the first time he'd ever eaten at Subway or seen food before. He didn't know what bread he wanted and was shocked that he actually got to choose. Seriously pal, have you ever eaten a sandwich? They have different types of bread. Look at what they are and decide the one you like best. You aren't choosing a soul mate.

Finally it's my turn. I order what I want and the lady frowns, offering a scolding reminder that what I selected isn't one of the five dollar specials, which I already knew since the only items on the five dollar special menu are things no one would want anyway. I understand it isn't on the five dollar menu. Can I have it anyway? I then argue for a minute that I don't want it toasted. Then I ask for extra tomatoes. That's an additional charge. Really? That would make sense if they didn't consider three wilted tomato slices to be standard for a sub.

When it's finally over I pay with a twenty. The lady marks it with a pen to see if it's counterfeit. I didn't realize Midge the sandwich artist was also a special agent. Like what would she do if it was fake, pull a lever that drops a net from the ceiling and holds me until the authorities get there?

As I'm leaving a woman behind me placed her order and then goes outside because she forgot her purse. Now the guy behind her is forced to wait even longer. As I'm leaving we lock eyes and I understand his concerns. He's been victimized by an Idiot too.

Have you ever been to a Japanese Hibachi Steakhouse? If you want to get a group of Idiots together all in one place, this is the place for you. What can be more exciting than having a chef toss around pieces of zucchini on a flaming stove drenched in hot butter, before rifling them into your mouth with a spatula? Where else can you go and have someone mock you in a foreign tongue then charge way too much for average food?

So we all sit like good little Americans around the excitement, close enough to potentially be set ablaze as the chef (who's really just a clown in a chef's hat) splatters flammable sake and oil all over a lava hot surface. I take mental note of all the huge grins plastered on everyone's face as they stare at the fire as though they've never seen one before. I'd be willing to wager if this same group of Idiots were sitting in their kitchen eating and a fire spit up in the air, they wouldn't be grinning.

So if that doesn't catch your eye, you may be interested in watching the many mystery juices that are squirted out onto your food from various ketchup bottles. One is brown. One is tinted yellow. What the hell is this stuff? I'm guessing it's not all natural ingredients from the springs of Fuji Mountain.

And then comes the butter. The chef (who speaks broken English, but goes by the name is Eric) has whipped the crowd into such a frenzy at this point by introducing a toy that urinates MSG all over your food that you don't notice he crammed three sticks of butter into the pile of shrimp. Is that the point of the peeing trinket? To distract you from the millions of calories and fat being added to your meal? Who cares right? As he puts it to the hysterical laughter of the crowd, it's "Yummy in your tummy!"

The flames are flying and the chef is really starting to go to town by playing with all the food, which appears to be entertaining every Idiot at the table. Onions are mimicking a choo choo train. An eruption of soy sauce is playing volcano. An egg is dropped onto a razor sharp Ginsu and split in half. What the hell is going on here? Am I at dinner or a circus?

And whatever you do, don't go on your birthday. The chef's will put some ancient bondage mask on your head and sing in a language no one understands, while some other fool shows up with a loud drum pounding it with no rhythm. When the mask comes off you get drowned with sake. It doesn't matter how old you are or if you are driving. Prepare to get sloshed.

The biggest surprise of the night isn't the flying zucchini. It's not the choo choo train with diced shrimp as the locomotive and a caboose of broccoli. It's the bill. Did I actually just spend $30 for a $5 plate of food? Yup! Was I thoroughly entertained? Maybe just a little. Does that mean I'm an Idiot? Or does it just mean I was force fed three bottles of sake?

"I like showing off a little bit at the grill table. I have been to these places once or twice before so I have practiced catching food in my mouth. Is it an unfair advantage? Probably. But I look, dare I say, cool." ~ Dirk – New Hartford, NY.

"My favorite part is the onion choo choo train. Not only do I feel like I'm sitting next to a real train, I feel like I am part of the show! It sort of makes me feel like I am on Broadway. Or that I'm an engineer!" ~ Baxter – Newark, NJ.

"I once went by myself. I wanted to try it out. It sucked. I had to sit with a dozen complete strangers at a birthday party. Never again." ~ "Friendless" Frank – Santa Fe, NM.

V

"Social" media in a world of Idiots

Social networks and social networking have created a generation of people that are, ironically, socially inept.

**Fact: 4.2 billion people use mobile devices for Social Media sites
Idiot Fact: Most of those people are annoying on Social Media.**

A decade ago, MySpace launched the fad of social networking and greatly changed the way every Tom, Dick, and Idiot goes about their lives. Since then, the torch has been passed to Facebook and Twitter, and as people read this book thousands of years from now, there will be some new phenomenon. While great for keeping touch with family and friends, why hang out and talk to people you like when you can sit home and text or message those you don't like? These social networking sites have created a new breed of human that has a complete lack of social skills and no ability to communicate offline.

The beginning of the end was born with the ability to use a phone for everything other than speaking. It's quicker, easier, and more convenient to send a text message than it is to actually call someone. Most phone companies now offer free talking because they know if they charged anything no one would make a single call. I think even E.T. would have texted the mother ship if provided the opportunity. Everyone would prefer texting, myself included (hey, I'm an Idiot too.)

The success and popularity of social networks has rapidly brought about a decline in actual conversation and tact. The complete destruction of mankind as we know it is Facebook. No other entity has been a more destructive force affecting the way people interact with each other.

On Facebook, everyone is a star. You have followers. You have thousands of friends. Many users use it as an excuse for garnering attention with nonsensical status updates or to pick fights with complete strangers. If your uncle died, I'm truly sorry, but don't broadcast it. If you think the President is ruining your life, great, stop complaining and feeling sorry for yourself. Do something about it other than posting something silly and watching your followers reply and argue with each other. This is what I like to call cyber-fueled road rage. Everyone is tough and mighty when slouching on their couch in the safety of their home with a laptop resting on their knees and a bag of chips off to the side. If it's something you wouldn't have the courage to say to someone else in person, you're an Idiot if you post it on Facebook.

"I don't like that O-Bamer. He's trying to take my guns and make us like Chiner." ~ Bufford – an avid wearer of overalls.

"My great grandmother died. She was ninety-eight, it was a total shock. I posted the updates so I could get sympathy from my Facebook friends." ~ Monica – a Bee keeper, Binghamton, NY.

Everyone who's anyone has a Facebook page, even businesses. Like I really want to be friends online with H&R Block. And news flash...no one should have more than 150 friends. And that's being generous. I don't think I've even spoken to 150 different people in my entire life. Maybe it's because I write stuff like this book. And please stop with the updates. No one cares that you are hungry or have a headache. Go eat a sandwich and pop an Advil.

"I have over 2,000 friends. Mostly guys. I like to make posts about what I'm doing and read their comments ☺ too bad most of them live halfway across the country ☹" ~ Erica – Utica, MI.

"Thinking about...chocolate..." ~ Sarah – a person whose life makes about as much sense as her status updates.

"I like informing my friends that I have a headache. That way when they text me they don't expect me to reply like really quick or whatever." ~ Brooke – second in charge cheerleader who would be first if Maria weren't so damned perky (Brooke's words, not ours.)

And Twitter is just as bad. On Twitter, you don't have friends, you have followers. Actually, you have neither you Idiot. Stop checking in at every restaurant you go to. Oh great, Jeff is at Taco Bell. I'd better stop playing video games and go meet him, even though he didn't invite me. Everyone from bands to poets has a Twitter page because it's really important for me to know that you're working on a new song. Just record it already so I can illegally download it.

"I have followers and they follow me. They like following me and I like that they like following me. I'm pretty cool and important." ~ JR Ripley – an absolute no one.

"I'm just grabbing a quick coffee...hold on I need to check in." ~ Some Idiot we decided wasn't worth interviewing.

Another caveat of Facebook or twitter pages is the uniqueness and individuality of the profile pic. This is designed so that all of your 28,800 friends can see how nifty you are. Men without shirts flexing pecs they don't have, making a face like they need to poop and punch a wall at the same time. Girls with hundreds of different self-shots, all of which feature them dressed in the same trashy outfit alone in their bedroom.

"It's like honey, if you were all that you'd be out with your boyfriend right now instead of hiding out in your room dressed like a floozy and listening to Adele. Mmmm mmmm snap snap." ~ Galloway Young – male fashion designer.

"I'm tough. I want my enemies to know who they can fear. Even though I don't approve my enemies friend requests. This way my friends no how tough I am so if any of my enemies are friends with my friends they may see the pic if they are at their house or whatever." ~ Tyler E – ice pond hockey goalie.

"I like to pucker my lips like I'm sucking on a lemon. Then I stare off into space, away from the camera. Talk about h-o-t HOT! ~ Jackie – high school freshman.

As much as I hate the camera hog, I hate the camera shy people as well. Why go through the trouble of setting up a Facebook page just to have a pic of your dog or favorite cartoon character or an out of focus pic with a group of fifty other people that you're hiding in like friggin Waldo.

"I have an important job. I only use the Facebook to talk to my family. That's why I don't have a profile pic." ~ Louise – someone with a job too important to tell us.

Then there are the old folks who set up a page. Nothing is cooler than having something in common with my Aunt Ester! But most of these old codgers take a year or so just to learn how to upload a photo. Grandma's profile pic is her at Christmas dinner. Nice to see it for the first time in mid-July.

By the way, does it make me an Idiot if I get mad when my friends list goes down and I don't know who removed me? Come on, you know that bugs you too.

The future is here and there's no stopping it now. I wish we could go back to the days when an app was actually a cool way of referring to an appetizer.

VI
Idiots in Public

Bathrooms

Fact: The average person spends 3 years of their life on the toilet. Idiot Fact: People don't like sitting on a public toilet seat.

Public bathrooms are full of complete Idiots. There are few simple rules one can follow while using a public restroom. In no particular order, but equally as important they are:

- No talking to your neighbor at a urinal
- Flush the toilet
- Don't pee on the seat
- Wash your hands

Idiots use public bathrooms and have complete disregard for everyone else but themselves. Is it that hard to make sure everything gets into a toilet? Is it that hard to then flush it? Do you have a good reason for not washing your hands? Others have to use the restroom too!

You would think that everyone could follow those simple rules, but they can't. Do you ever notice that every time you enter a bathroom and someone is in a stall, you hear them start to cough, sniffle or clear their throat? It must be some sort of animal instinct to let people know: "Hey everyone, I am crapping in here so don't swing my door open." You would think a closed stall door with feet sitting there would be enough, but it isn't. The person still feels the need to send out warning signals.

"Hey Pal; I know you're in there. You don't need to set road flares and launch fireworks to get my attention. I won't come in. Promise! Besides, don't you lock the stall door?"

And you know they can hear you enter the bathroom, because for some reason bathrooms amplify your feet to sound like you are wearing tap dancing shoes. If anyone needs foot step sounds for a movie, hang out in the bathroom with a recording device. I always feel like I am a special agent walking around. Well in this case, a special agent who needs to use the bathroom.

Have you ever been in a stall that didn't have a lock, but you had no choice but to use it anyway? How stressful is that? You have to hold the door as if some intruder is going to try and storm their way in. You try and reach out with your hand or make a half-assed effort to reach the door with your foot to hold it shut, all while being completely stressed out.

Now that you have been warned, what do you do next if you too, need to use a stall? Do you proceed to the one next to them or do you retreat? As much fun as it is to sit next to someone with your pants around your ankles passing gas, you're probably going to want to avoid that situation altogether. How do you do it, you ask? You need to make a split decision. Some people head for a urinal, to the sink to wash their hands or better yet, they just retreat.

"Those options sound good. Tell me more." When you walk in and hear the coughs and sniffles, immediately head for a urinal even if you don't have to go. This can be tricky, because if you don't have to go and it is quiet in there, you will be caught. Sure, you can flush the toilet to cover up the sound of silence, but the water will stop and it will be quite evident that you never started.

Don't worry; you do have other options. How about washing your hands? You have two hands right? Why not wash them? Do you know that you have a 50% chance of looking credible in this situation? We did the math. Think about it, you could have been eating a gyro for lunch and had to wash that white sauce off of your hands, right? The problem, however, is that the person in the stall probably doesn't buy it. But what if you just always carry a gyro in your pocket just in case you need it for the bathroom? Good idea? Maybe as you are walking in you could start talking to yourself about how good the gyro was and that you really need to wash your hands etc...?

Did you ever leave the bathroom and your hands are still wet after washing? It can be pretty uncomfortable if you run into someone who wants to shake your hand immediately. You feel like you have to explain in great detail that it is water on your hands. "I swear I didn't pee all over my hands, I swear!"

The last option you have is what I like to call, "The Houdini exit." The Houdini exit will make you feel like a magician and it will make the person in the stall happiest.

When you walk in and notice something isn't right, you simply back pedal or moonwalk out of the bathroom, letting the door close in front of you. It will appear to the person in the stall that the door just opened and shut, but no one is in the bathroom. How could that be? How did someone open the door and just vanish? A good magician never reveals his tricks and that is exactly what you are… a good magician. Not only will you be glad, but the person in the stall will be too.

Going into the bathroom and picking a stall is basically like playing the game show "Let's make a deal." What will be behind stall #1? Perhaps a dirty seat? Maybe it looks like a tornado tore through? No toilet paper? Why do some Idiots leave the bathroom without flushing? Is it that hard to push the lever down with your foot? Emphasis on the foot. Have you ever seen writing on the walls at work? Aren't we adults? This is a Fortune 500 company; do you really need to express your love for Cassandra by writing it on the wall in marker?

Have you ever been going to the bathroom when the cleaning guy comes in? How awkward is that? While you are doing your business, this guy is wandering around like nothing is going on. Occasionally you will see a mop go sliding by your feet. Come on pal, can you wait a second? And what is he thinking? He has to be somewhat embarrassed right?

And I'm all for equality but how annoying is it when you're in the stall and there's a soft tapping on the door from some old woman who wants to clean? Now I have to yell "WAIT!!!! I'm IN HERE!!!" The cough and sniffles aren't going to work on this part time retiree. The awkwardness continues as I finish up, wash, and leave, only to find her standing outside waiting. "Is there anyone else in there?" She asks. "Um…I don't think so. Not sure." I reply, even though I know damn well it was just me. Next time she knocks, I swear I'm going to say, "Come on in!" That'll show her.

And do we really need bathroom attendants? What the hell purpose do they serve, and more importantly, who thought up that job in the first place? Was there a CEO somewhere who was pointing to a chart in a meeting saying: "There is a big untapped market aimed at people that are going to the bathroom. We need to get some products in there and get them there fast. Watkins, get some Starburst and head to the nearest restaurant bathroom. Offer them some hairspray. Yes yes…Turn the water on for them. Hand them a towel. Stand over their shoulder. Breathe down their necks. People like that!" They act like we just walked into a bathroom and completely forgot how to use our hands. Thanks for handing me a paper towel square, but I think I can figure that out on my own. Then you have to stand there drying your hands as they watch you. All the while you are thinking to yourself how you can walk out of there without tipping him. Of course you feel guilty, but I'd rather just dry my hands off with my dollar bills than give them away. Did you ever spritz on some cologne from one of those guys? Me neither. Since when did shopping get added to your trip to the bathroom?

I can't help to wonder how many people actually wash their hands, especially when no one else is in the bathroom to see them. We asked a couple of people to see what they do when they go to the public restroom.

"It's cold in the bathroom and the last thing I want to do is put my hands in water. No way, no how, not gonna do it. I choose to fake wash my hands instead. Sometimes I just run the water and put my hands near the faucet, but that is only to fake someone else out who is in there. Otherwise, I just walk out." ~ Fergie - Palm Springs, CA.

"I would wash my hands only if I ate a hot pepper sandwich and deuced. Not one or the other. I have to do both. Then I may wash." ~ Dip Smith - Milwaukee, WI

"I usually just get a really mean look on my face and storm out of there. This way, if someone questions me, they are asking for a fight." ~T Bone Harris – Steak enthusiast.

"Depends Depends Depends. It's not worth missing a pitch at a ball game." ~ Marty – Florence, SC.

"I hate when people standing next to me start talking to me. In this case I usually zip up while I am still in the process of going. I just want to get out of there and that seems like a logical plan. This obviously leaves me no time to wash, but that is the last thing on my mind." ~ Billy – Billings, MT.

Have you ever gone to grab the bathroom door and it flies open almost breaking your wrist? Behind the door of course, an Idiot has pressed the automatic handicapped door opener. As an adult, do you really need to pretend you are Obi-Wan Kenobi using the force to open a door?

Idiots will argue that it's more sanitary than using the door handle. But since almost everyone thinks that way, and therefore uses the handicap button instead of the actual door handle, that theory goes out the window now doesn't it.

Shaking my head and entering, I immediately scare some other Idiot who is checking his teeth out in the mirror. He looks back like he's up to no good and fixes his hair quickly then leaves. No one is buying it pal. Everyone knows you were checking yourself out. Allow me to save you the time; you look like a fool.

Ever spend a good five minutes arranging the seat cover and get ready to sit and hear WOOOSH!? Hey, where did my seat cover go? The automatic toilet has flushed it away. ☹ This can happen several times before you finally are able to fool it long enough to sit down and do your business. The electronic flush, turns into electronic everything else that doesn't work. Now I'm all for the environment but the amount of towel released by the automatic towel machines is ridiculous. They produce a spec so small I need at least 3 or 4 to actually dry my hands, thus I end up exerting more energy by activating the machine half a dozen times than if I was just allowed to get my own towels. And why is it that I am not allowed to get my own towels? Because bathroom owners know everyone acts like an Idiot in the bathroom.

"People will have no problem putting their hands under an air dryer for ten minutes in a bathroom only to go temporarily deaf and then find out that their hands are still wet" ~ Inventor of the bathroom hand dryer.

Why is it that every once in a while you will see someone in the bathroom practically bathing themselves? Did you ever walk in and see someone rinsing their head? Is it part of their job description to run a marathon in the morning? I can't see any other reason for them needing to dunk their head in the sink. Sometimes I even see a sign that says, "No Smoking." Really? In this day and age do we really need to alert smokers that they can't smoke in a bathroom? Do some of them mistake a public bathroom for outside?

"I hate when I am picking at my face or teeth and someone swings open the door. It is a public restroom, but at least they should knock first." ~ Barry– An avid fan of privacy.

"I don't wash my hands because there are so many germs on the sink. Besides, they are just going to get dirty again anyway." ~ Aaron - Portland, OR

"There isn't enough time in the day. I use the bathroom at the end of the day to brush my teeth and wash-up a little. If I am going out, I change in the stall. I hate stepping on the floor with bare feet, but it saves time." ~ Simon - Montreal, CA

Sneaker Store

Fact: that the word "sneaker" comes from "sneaking around"?
Idiot Fact: A lot of people have ugly smelly feet.

Ever been to a sneaker store? Every now and then I go shopping for running sneakers. I prefer to try on my sneakers, so unfortunately I have to go to the sneaker store and can't just get them online like everything else.

I have a special way of knowing when I need to get a new pair. When I run in mine, they provide no support; they don't smell the best and look like I walked in a swamp. So after calculating all of that on my own, I have decided it's off to the sneaker store. I get a little nervous going to get new sneakers, because I really don't want someone who took the job with no prior foot experience, to be fondling my feet. I know my size and can put my own shoe on thank you very much. Measuring really isn't that hard. You put your foot on the black metal measuring thingamabopper and open your eyes to read what it says.

The problem with sneaker stores is they never seem to have your size. It never fails. A sneaker is on sale and it looks decent. There is no way they have it. If I'm a size 10, rest assured they have a surplus of 7's 8's 9's 11's 12's and of course the ever so obnoxious 10.5's. In fact, the only size 10 is the bright green high-tops named after the most current NBA star. They come complete with pillow pump cloud sole and blinding orange laces. I think I'll pass.

The first challenge is trying to get one of the employees to actually pay attention to you. Let's face it; they really don't feel like touching your feet as much as you don't want them to. They usually hang around near the T-Shirts that they are selling for $40. Does anyone ever buy one of those? I feel like they are just there for show. Who is going to pay $40 for a Knicks T-shirt when you can get it for $7 at a department store?

After an hour of flagging down one of the teen Idiots, I ask for a size 11. The employee then goes in the back for what seems like hours. In your mind, you know damn well they don't have it. So what are they going to bring you? A cake? Perhaps a bologna sandwich? There is no telling what they are up to back there. I mean the store is the size of my bathroom. How big could the back room be? Did they leave a bread crumb trail so they could find their way out?

Twenty minutes goes by as I stand around like an Idiot in my socks. That is another story all together. Do my socks stink? Are they dirty? Are they the same? How many holes do they have? Out comes the Idiot holding two boxes. Great, I only asked for one sneaker. He apologizes but reassures, they don't have an 11 but they do have a 7 and a 14. Then he asks if I want to try either of those on. Really, do I want to try one of those? Yes, let me give the 7 a try. I might be able to put my foot in a dryer and shrink it 4 sizes. That seems logical. Or better yet, let me try the 14. I will just fertilize my foot and feed it plenty of water.

"I like foot massages. Sometimes I just go to try on sneakers for the free foot touching. After I am done trying on six pairs I just grab my stuff and run full speed out of the store." ~ Garret. - Sock salesman.

Barbershop

Fact: An average person gets 9.35 haircuts per year.
Idiot Fact: Most barbers don't know how to cut hair.

Going to the barber should be an enjoyable time? It should, but not when the shop is filled with a bunch of Idiots. And it's not just the patrons; it can be the staff too. I go to a place where you have to take a number. Seems easy enough right? You walk in, take a number, sit down and read the newspaper until you hear it called. Quite simplistic actually, at least you would think, but it is actually the most nerve racking experience you can go through, aside from sharing a bread basket at a restaurant.

I'm sitting there waiting for my usual barber that I trust and my number gets called. "Number 30!" says Fozzio the owner. Why do the barbershop owners always have weird names and abnormal hairstyles?

"I have 30 and I am waiting for Jackie." I say as I sit filled with anxiety as I will most likely get the blind barber who uses a chainsaw to cut hair. Oh, and not to mention probably offend the other barbers as I give the impression that I think they don't know what the hell they are doing.

So they take my number and ask who else is next. Someone else says they are waiting for Bobbi the hair dresser, so they take their number and then take the next person. As you can imagine, I know for darn sure they have just screwed up the process and will forget I am waiting for Jackie. I was already waiting for a half an hour and now know I will have to speak up when some idiot tries to say he is next. Into the barbershop, steps an Idiot with his kid who looks like a little nerd. I can already tell this guy wants everyone's full attention on him.

"We are going to Disney World so cut his hair short." Says the father. What does going to Disney World and a short haircut have to do with each other? He obviously wanted the whole room to know he was going to Disney World, as if we care. I just care about not getting skipped. So the father is waiting as his son gets his hair cut.

"Number 33!"say's Fozzio. Jackie is now open and the father tries to slip in my spot. "Son of a...!" I thought. So, I intervene." Sorry I was waiting for Jackie." I said. The 45+ year old father now has a completely puzzled look on his face, unlike when he was talking about Disney World. It was as if his whole Disney World came crashing down. Goofy, Pluto, Mickey, everyone!

"What number did you have?" said Fozzio who took my number 10 minutes earlier. "30, I was waiting for Jackie." I replied as I could clearly see their number system had failed miserably. Oh, before I forget, they also had two 29s in the number set. Everyone knows you are only supposed to have one 29. Two 29s is downright absurd, back to my story. The fear starts to set in that if I don't get Jackie, who knows what someone else will do to my hair. Will Wilma the new recruit just start cutting like there is no tomorrow? She has already been making references to being out late drinking the night before. Great! And here is the best part. The father interjects. "No worries Fozzio, I will wait... Really, don't worry about it." "What?!?" Don't worry about it? I was first. What is there to worry about? Why are you playing cool as if you are taking the higher road?

Luckily all is well as Jackie finally cuts my hair. Of course she wants to talk about nonsense and I don't. I don't care that you are painting your shed, just pay attention to what you are doing. You have a sharp metal object dancing around my head. This isn't a chance to make small talk or host your own home improvement talk show. I have been going there, once a month, for a couple of years and we start the conversation off the same way every time. "Do you have kids? You do? What are their names?" That, they can't remember and then they get pissed if you remind them how you want your hair cut. As if it is an insult. She ends up cutting it wrong in the end anyway. I should have tried drunken Wilma this time.

A Idiot?

Post Office

Fact: The Postal Service handles 43% of the world's mail.
Idiot Fact: The Post Office employs lots of interesting characters.

So who uses the post office anymore? Idiots, that's who. With email and texting and online bill pay, it's no wonder why post offices are going under everywhere. I feel bad, but come on. The average postal worker makes fifty grand a year to be a glorified paperboy with government funded benefits and a hundred or so vacation days a year, no wonder the national debt is so high.

When I say the words Post Office, do you cringe? I do. Why, when I have to mail something that I can't fit in the mailbox do I have to rearrange my day? I usually end up canceling plans so I can stand in line for a couple of hours. It just doesn't make any sense to me. Grocery store cashiers can ring up $300 dollars of groceries, bag them, even sell stamps and then run your credit card in far less time than a postal worker can print out a label to put on a box. I guess I shouldn't be that critical, they do also have to ask you if you put any kryptonite or grenades in your package. Has anyone ever put that stuff in there and then said yes when asked? Are there any hazardous items in the box that is the size of a CD case? "Yes actually, in that tiny box I have placed broken glass, acid, a full sized tank of gas and a loaded canon that can shoot a circus clown across a room." Are we to believe criminals and terrorists will buckle under pressure when asked by a slow paced clerk? Are they that stupid?

My favorite is how a postal worker will watch you place a t-shirt in a package and still ask you that question. As if you are David Copperfield and can change the contents of that package before their very eyes. "Well, I am glad you asked... the T-shirt you saw me put in the package has turned into an alligator. You might not want to hold on to that one too long." And could you have more inconvenient hours? Seriously, Mon-Fri 10-4. Sorry, like everyone else I'm working during that time. Even postal workers are "working."

Have you ever been in a Post Office when there isn't a line? Ha, that's funny. I am guessing the only time there isn't one, is when a tornado is ripping through the area. If that happens, you may have a small window to get in and get out in less than an hour with some stamps. Stamps...They are just stickers for big kids. I was behind a lady who was spending 10 minutes trying to figure out what stamps she wanted for her Christmas cards. "Hmm, which will Hal like better, the snowman or the Santa stamp?" I got news for you, Hal doesn't give a damn what is on the outside of your letter. You will be lucky if he even notices the stamp. It may just go directly from the mailbox into the garbage, but thanks for being so thoughtful.

Elevators

Fact: Elevators are twenty times safer than escalators.
Idiot Fact: Elevators don't like it when you fart inside them.

Elevators might be the smallest public place you will ever be in. You can't escape even though you may really want to. The more packed it gets, the more you want out. Ever been standing nose to nose with someone trying to look elsewhere? It's not very easy to do. You are basically forced to start counting nose hairs until the door opens. Forget about if someone rips one. There is nowhere to go. Did you ever get on an empty elevator and it smells as if the elevator passed gas? Each person who rides handles each situation differently.

If the elevator stops on every floor, it can really set some people off. You would think that it just tacked on 3 hours to their commute by the way they act. Some of them are breathing hard and shuffling around to let you know that they are upset. Others just sit there and deal with it. I have seen a few people's heads just explode in frustration. Odors can be tough too. Some people feel the need to put on a quart of perfume, seemingly rub deodorant all over the place or in some cases just not bathe.

Ever run into someone you don't feel like talking to on an elevator? (Besides always) How awkward is that? You start talking about the weather and other forced conversation. You better hope it isn't a long ride, because the weather conversation can only last so long. You may be forced to get as specific as talking about dew points.

And news flash, hitting a button more than once, or with force doesn't make the doors close any faster or the ride take any less time.

"I always quickly hit the close doors button so the door shuts faster. Everyone around me thinks I am a hero for giving them 2 seconds more on their day." ~ Gordo a vegetable enthusiast.

"If I have to pass gas in an elevator so be it. I am not waiting to get off and do it. It is a natural thing and everyone does it. Did you ever read that book "Everyone Poops?" ~ Harrison- a selfish fool.

"I always hope a hot chick gets on with me and the elevator breaks down. I've seen it on TV. I'll save her by climbing through the top part and climbing the ropes to another floor and forcing the doors open. Then I'll reach my hand down and pull her to safety and we'll kiss and be together forever. ~ William – A man who watches too much TV.

Convenient Stores

Fact: The top selling item in convenience stores is tobacco.
Idiot Fact: The other top items include beer and lottery tickets.
(Great habits!)

Idiots make convenience stores anything but convenient. I run into the convenient store to grab a few gallons of water. I buy water okay, deal with it. I smile because there is only one person in front of me in line. But my excitement is short lived when I notice the guy has no purchases - he is clutching a fistful of scratch off tickets, each one a complete loser, just like he is. I hope it's just a short encounter but my intellect tells me it won't be. The man rudely tosses the losing tickets on the counter and expects the cashier to dispose of them for him. The scratch shavings are all over the place. I'm actually surprised he doesn't just throw them on the ground. He then methodically begins selecting more tickets. This Idiot has a system. He knows which tickets will win (though to date he hasn't won anything). I begin shifting the handful of gallon jugs I have. Come on Asshole, hurry up with your stupid tickets!

After sorting through the bevy of options he has his tickets and is preparing for a life of sitting on the beach. He's not going to retire early because he clearly doesn't work anyway - he just wants to sit on the beach. He's finally done. Or is he? He then begins to stand at the counter scratching off the tickets one by one.

And he even has a system for this act as well, as if it matters which order he scratches them off in. I readjust the gallons of water, and make eye contact with the cashier. It seems he's a regular. What an Idiot. That would be like me buying a Snapple and standing at the counter drinking it.

He finishes and alleluia, he has won $2!!!!! Not bad for a $10 investment. Rather than take his winnings, he decides to purchase two more one dollar tickets. This Idiot isn't planning on leaving until he has no money left. And that is exactly what happens.

"If I have an extra dollar, I am spending it. No if ands or but's. I like the thrill of winning. Too bad that never happens. You can't stop me though. I am gonna win big I tells ya. BIG!" ~ Randy – a man who never wins at lotto.

Wine Stores

Fact: One glass of wine is drunk for every three bottles of beer. Idiot Fact: One drunk wino is one too many.

You can find plenty of Idiots in and around wine stores. Whether it is the clerk at the counter who would make love to grapes if he could, shoppers who have no clue what they are looking for or simply a passed out drunk laying near the entrance, you get a wide variety of folks.

We can start with the store clerk, who is usually soft spoken and seems to have tried every wine made to man. This in layman's terms means: Wino or Drunk. We always ask his advice as if he has the same taste buds and likes as us. Why don't I ask the stocker at a grocery store how the Rice Krispy's taste? Well maybe I will!

"What do you recommend?" We usually ask as we are basically handing over our wallets and letting them spend our money for us. And after you ask for their recommendation, you are over committed and can't take a step back. It's not like you can say, thanks for your recommendation of the $20 bottle, but I am going to buy the $3 bottle instead.

Oh and I don't want to hear about the grapes, where they came from, who picked them, stomped on them or what storms past over them while they grew. I don't care. Does it taste good, will I look like a cheap ass bringing this bottle and is the price right? Those are the questions I want answered. That and the most important of all; will I get a good buzz?

"I won't touch anything but 18th century merlot bottled in Versailles. Not a drop of anything else. Not one drop I say." ~ Frederick Snobsville.

Movie Theater

Fact: The average American eats nearly 70 quarts of popcorn a yr. Idiot Fact: The average American should not eat that much popcorn.

I like to go to the movies from time to time, but for some reason a movie with the public turns into a big production in itself. I am always afraid that if I get to the theater too late that all of the good seats will be taken and I will have to look sideways and straight up to see the movie. That is why I get there way too early, which also is annoying.

You know what else is annoying, the price of candy in a theater. How do they justify charging $75 for Milk Duds? $55 for Skittles? With prices like that, I find it my duty as an American to fight back. There is only one thing you can do; you must sneak in your own. How ridiculous is it that at the age of 35, you have to sneak a pack of starburst past the teenage security? Of course to do so, I concoct this well thought out plan, only to walk right past them with no problem at all. Maybe it was the fake mustache I was wearing. I don't know, but I made it.

Now that I think about it, I have no idea why I wore a fake mustache at all. As I make my way to the theater to watch the 40 advertisements and 25 previews before the main show. Of course I am there extra early, so I don't have a choice. As soon as the theater fills up and the lights go down, one hefty lady comes lumbering in and takes the seat next to me. Do us all a favor, if you don't get there on time, leave and get a ticket for another showing. She sits next to me eating a hot dog and I can smell the disgusting ketchup, whipped crème and whatever other garbage she has put on it. Since when did a movie theater become a ball park? Why do you have to eat a bunch of crap when you watch a movie? If I get something on Netflix I don't sit on my couch with a 3 liter bottle of cola and a king sized box of junior mints or a hot dog.

Some movies are must see movies in the theater. If they have special effects, that's the place to see it. Some people get really upset if you didn't see a movie. "Are you kidding me, you haven't seen it yet? How could you not have seen it yet? It's a classic." Easy, I didn't see the damn movie... that is how. People seem to take it so personally. On the flip side, people seem to get mad if you see movies. "You saw that? It looked terrible from the previews. How could you do that?" I don't know how many times people say the book was much better. Great, so don't watch the movie then. I don't need to hear you complain about it. I get it, you have a great imagination. Maybe even a better one than the director.

I always hear people complaining on how expensive movies are getting. Then don't go. Those same people end up buying books for more money than the movie and have to do work to get through it. How come they never complain about how much the book is?

"I didn't think Edward would have looked like that. The book had him looking differently." ~ Grace - someone who obviously doesn't understand that the producer of the movie doesn't care what she thinks Edward should look like.

Grocery Store

Fact: The #1 item people buy at a grocery store is Bread.
Idiot Fact: Some people go to the grocery store to try and get a date.

One of my least favorite things to do is grocery shop, because when I go, I know I am about to pick up a bunch of items that I don't really need. In my head, I can go to the store, spend $50 and come out with a weeks' worth of healthy food. In reality, I buy a few things and walk out $200 later and always ask myself: "How could I have possibly spent that much?" But, somehow we convince ourselves that beer, Doritos and ice cream are a necessity.

Even when I make a list it doesn't work. I write down lunch and dinner for every night of the week. Then in the store, my stomach starts acting like a bully. "I'm still going to be hungry after eating that you know. You should really get more. Get some chips you wimp. What are you a pansy? Throw some beer in that cart." So I do.

Driving to the store is one thing; parking when you get there is another. There are never parking spots available close to the store. It seems as if the grocery store owns 200 cars that it places in all of the good spots, because they never seem to move. While looking for a parking spot, I also have to dodge 10 carts that are lying all over the place. Are people that lazy that they can't bring a cart back to one of those cart stations? You only have to walk 20 feet to find one of them. Some people decide it is easier to just park their cart in a parking space. That makes sense right? A parking space is for cars, so that means you should park a shopping cart in it? With that logic, gasoline is for gas tanks, so I am going to just pour this sugar into your gas tank. Not really though, because I never buy sugar.

And all it takes is one Idiot leaving a cart wherever they want to start the madness. Just one. Then the next Idiot has all intentions of putting the cart where it belongs, but what do they do? They see the one cart in the middle of the lot and think to themselves "The cart guy is going to have to get that cart anyway; I might as well leave mine there too." The next Idiot does the same thing, and the madness is on. Carts here, carts there, carts are everywhere. I've even seen people push the cart farther away than it would have been to just bring it back to the store. I've even seen some upside down, which is nearly impossible to do. How did they do that?

"Sometimes if I don't feel like it, I just leave my shopping cart in the middle of the parking lot. It is way easier than putting the cart back where it belongs, plus I save time." ~ Hector – retired coupon cutter

"I hate when people drive SUV's to the grocery store. Did you ever try and park next to one of them? It's nearly impossible. That is why I just take up two spots. That will teach those jerks." – Frank

Did you ever have to hold the door for someone at a supermarket? I never knew how awkward it could be just going through a door. For some reason I feel obligated to hold the door for the person behind me. What am I, a bellhop at the Hilton? I don't feel obligated to cook the fries for the guy behind me at Burger King so why do I need to open the door for a perfectly healthy man. And if I stop to make the effort to hold the door and I don't get a "thanks," it's on!

How about when someone's behind you – not close enough to hold the door but just far enough not to let it go. You smile politely as you stand there holding it in this lose-lose situation. The person behind you either pretends not to see you (which is what I would do) or they start to jog to get there quickly, thus becoming an Idiot.

"I'd rather not hold the door for someone. It cuts into my day and I got things to do." ~ Charles who is currently unemployed and was fired for being impolite.

"I get so nervous wondering if I should hold the door. Sometimes I don't know what to do and I just pretend I am on the phone." ~ Ken – Yogurt enthusiast

Have you ever gotten a good sale item? Where do they let you know of these deals? Every time I go down the aisle, I see a sale on something that I want, only to find that the shelf has been cleaned out and it looks like a tornado ripped through. "Lobster for a nickel." The tank is empty except for a rubber band at the bottom. Cereal for $.25, shelf is bare, but every other brand is there. I feel like its Black Friday and no one told me about it. Then there are about four other shoppers there too, looking at the shelf like a natural disaster took place.

It's like escaping from Alcatraz getting out of that situation. Old ladies are walking around clueless with carts blocking the whole area. Others grip coupons and look defeated.

"I read labels and it makes me feel much better if I read them out loud. Eating organic shows everyone else that I have a lot more money than them and how I am in tune with healthy choices. I don't even know what half of it means, but I sound like I do." ~ Veronica – Insect watcher

"Sometimes I just stroll up and down the frozen food aisle arguing with the cable company. What? Their rates are way too high!" ~ General Joe – retired Mall Cop

"The bottle return guy is a jerk. I had three freaking bottles from Switzerland that he said he couldn't take back. What a moron. I was so pissed I just smashed them in the parking lot." ~ Bart – Soap Opera extra

If you want to get out of the store on time and you want to talk to the least amount of people possible, don't bring a baby. Waiting at the deli counter can be more painful than the nitrates in the meat your about to buy. I recall waiting for some Swiss cheese and out of the corner of my eye I see a lady with a smile ear to ear looking at my daughter. I know if I make eye contact, I will have to tell her the usual information that every stranger asks. "How old is she?" "What is her name?" As if they are going to use that information for something later. Those questions are usually followed by uncomfortable conversations about people they know who have kids and what they are doing. As much as you think I would be interested in hearing what a stranger's nephew is doing, I really don't care. I didn't come to the deli counter to chat about tummy time or hear what kind of binky's your nephew uses. I really just want to get my cheese and get out of there. I didn't bring my daughter for an ice breaker and I don't want her to smell like your perfume. But really, thanks so much for saying hello; it means the world to me. And they always say how cute your kid is. Did you ever hear someone say? "Oh wow, she is just ugly as can be."

Once I have collected a bunch of items in my cart, it is off to the checkout. Of course, I have to dodge a few people in the aisle who are pretending to read the nutritional information. Half that stuff you need a chemist by your side to understand. Ah yes, Detestorucose syrup is in my crackers. That sounds good for me, I will get that. Here is a hint for you. If the food never goes bad, it probably isn't good for you.

As I finally make it to the cashier, a very helpful employee greets me with a couple of different options for purchasing my food. "You can make your way over to register 4, where Connie would love to assist you, or you can do the self-checkout." Thanks, like I couldn't figure out which checkout register will be available next. Hmmm self-checkout, there is a novel idea that puts people out of work. How often does the self-checkout work without calling over an employee to help you? The first screen nicely asks if you would like to cash out in German, Spanish, French and oh yeah English. Tough decision, seeing that we live in America. I usually go with English. Next I slide the bar code over the scanner about 25 times before it registers and place the item in the bag. At this point the machine yells at me for not putting it in the bag correctly, so I have to redo it and eventually call over the attendant. In the amount of time it takes me to self-checkout, I could have waited in a line behind someone who questions every item and coupon they are buying, only to write a check for the cashier. Who writes checks anymore? I don't even know how they work? Is it the honor system? Hi cashier lady, here is a piece of paper that is good for however much my groceries are. Good luck.

And some products appear to be the work of Idiots – or at least that's who they are marketing them to. Tide Extra Strength, and it's the same price and size as the regular Tide. Why wouldn't they just make all the Tide extra strength and get rid of the regular one?

Or pink SOS scrubs for "light duty messes" as if anyone has ever said they have a light duty mess to clean up.

Wide taco shells for putting stuff in. Again, why continue to make the old ones if the new is better and the same price?

And one of my favorite things about the grocery store is the generic products that are right next to the name brands, and are always cheaper. And they always have Idiotic names too. Instead of $4 for a box of Cocoa Krispies, you can pay $3 for the ever popular Chocolate Nuggets. Or instead of Oreos try the Cream Filled Circles. I love when they try to mimic the brand name mascot too. Everyone knows Tony the Tiger and Frosted Flakes, but have you met Jimmy the Puma and his oh so tasty Iced Pellets? Who is getting fooled by Jimmy's charm?

And when paying by credit card, does it really matter how I sign it? Like the signature matters. I scribble anything and they always accept. In stores they make you sign, but you could fill your car up with $2,000 worth of gas and not have to sign and no one is there to witness it – as long as you enter your zip code at the pump. I could just scribble, like I always do and they wouldn't know. One store had me sign with my finger tip and when I was finished it, it looked like Helen Keller wrote it.

I love the laws designed to prevent underage drinking. They check my ID with an infrared scanner and then I pay by credit card and they could care less if it's me or not. I like when they proof me when I'm buying a bottle of wine, as if some teenager with a fake ID would be buying a bottle of French merlot.

One time the clerk refused to sell me beer because I happened to walk in at the same time as some other guy (who I'd never seen before in my life) and they assumed we were together. What was really idiotic is that the other guy looked older than me. Like if a father is with his ten year old son do they refuse to sell beer to him?

And how Idiotic are brewery websites that make you enter your birth date in order to get in. Like really? Are there teenagers that are so stupid they enter their actual birth date and get blocked out? And by the way, who cares how old you are? It's a website not an actual keg.

When you are checking out, stores know it is a good time to try to get you to donate. "Sir would you like to donate $1 to kids with no knee caps?" Of course, if I choose not to donate, I feel like karma may come back to haunt me. What if I lose my knee caps because I didn't donate? Of course the cashier and the lady behind me make me feel so guilty I end up donating anyway. I guess that is okay, because I am a big believer in children having knee caps. As you can see, I didn't write about a real disease, because I didn't want karma to get me for joking about it. Or maybe someone who reads this will alert me that it is in fact real! If so, I will donate! Stop guilting me into it!

And why is it so embarrassing to buy condoms? You see people acting like James Bond, sneaking around to make sure no one else sees. Why does it matter? We all do it. And of course the self-checkouts are all down at the other end, so you have to go through a regular line. Would it be smarter to just keep having a bunch of kids instead of sneaking around to buy them? What is the cashier thinking when you slap them on the counter?

For some reason I feel like the clerk won't notice if I add a pack of gum to the purchase. Everyone is starring. It's like the pressure of walking into a small store and feeling obligated to buy something. I always pray there is someone else in there so I can make a clean getaway, like I'm going to offend the kid working the counter if I just leave. Let's not even bring up itchy cream or ointment. I always feel like I have to tell a story to the clerk and explain myself. Sometimes

I pretend I am on the phone talking to someone. "Hey Sullivan, I found the ointment you wanted... You know, the one that you wanted and it is not for me?" Of course then I realize Sullivan is a guy's name and I quickly have to cover that up, cause that sounds bad. "Yeah Sullivan, that ointment your wife wanted you to get, but then you called me because you knew I knew what ointment she was looking for."

Coffee Shops

Fact: Coffee is the second most traded commodity on earth.
Idiot Fact: For some reason people think they are cooler drinking coffee.

Coffee shops can be a great place to get a nice bold cup of coffee and relax. They can also be a magnet for some interesting and highly obnoxious Idiots. When going into a coffee shop, you will see a wide variety of people. Some people think they are screen writers creating the next film of the year. They have their laptops out on the tables, while they type away on their latest master piece. Others think they will be the next big author. (Just an FYI, we aren't typing this book in a coffee shop.)

Others think it is a library and read full books while other patrons patiently wait for a seat. Then you have people wearing suits who talk loudly so everyone can hear as they are making business deals. Do they really think we care that they are doing?

Don't people work anymore? Coffee shops always seem to be full at all times of the day with these people. Are we to believe that they all work at night? Is that why they are in the coffee shop...to load up on coffee to stay awake at night? Then again, since they are all aspiring writers, maybe the coffee shop is their office and they are at work...Maybe?

Waiting in line at a coffee shop is the worst. You have your group orders, where they send one fool out to get 30 coffees for the office. You could be standing one person away from ordering your plain coffee, when some Idiot pulls out a posted note. They begin to read off a bunch of orders, which you know will take a good hour to create.

Then you have your Idiot customers, they try and create the weirdest coffee they can. What is mocha, vanilla latte, with extra ice, light water and skim? Who orders that?

Or the girl who gets the Mocha java with sugar and extra whipped cream. Sweetheart, just go get a frosty at Wendy's. They hear that coffee is good for you on the news and try to convince themselves that it is a coffee. I guess maybe it has a coffee bean or two ground up in there with a side of 4 pounds of sugar and whipped crème.

I love when I pull into the drive thru and they try to sell me something I would never want. Like pretentious assholes (like me) who go to a coffee shop don't already know what they are getting since they get the same thing every day. I don't feel like trying a blueberry coffee today. Black coffee will be fine. I walk into a department store and I don't have to deal with some Idiot at the door trying to sell me a tacky sweater vest. And at Halloween time, every time I get a pumpkin iced coffee they ask if I would like to try a pumpkin donut too. What do they think I'm some pumpkin junkie?

And don't ever offer to make a coffee run. If you're getting five orders, you can bet on one thing; the first four will be simple...number five will be the Idiot who wants the medium mocha chai latte with whipped icing and East

African cinnamon on the top. And then you have to go back and deal with the awkward change distribution. Sammy had a latte. Here is your nickel Sammy. Brenda is the Idiot who didn't give me enough money for the low calorie milkshake she ordered, and Jake calls me out on not getting the right artificial sugar packet that causes diseases in mice.

There are other times when I get questioned like I am under investigation. I go to the coffee shop to get my usual large iced coffee black, and of course the girl with the nose ring has to ask "Isn't it too cold for iced coffee?" No honey, it's not. With that logic you couldn't have iced water, refrigerated milk, or soda during the winter. I would obviously have to wear a scarf so I don't freeze to death from the ice. And do you think she asks that to the Idiots ordering hot coffee in the summer? If you're stupid shop sells it, why is it so odd that people buy it? Why don't you question company headquarters?

And what's up with the tip jar? Like $4 for a cup of coffee isn't enough? You press a button on a register and I am supposed to give you a 25% tip? My mailman trudges through snow every day to bring me my mail. I have yet to see his tip jar. A crew of guys installed a fence in my backyard. It took them two days in 90 degree heat. No tip. Someone hands me a cup of coffee and you are begging for a tip? Although in a bar, I have no problem handing a dollar over without thinking about it for a pint of beer. It's a crazy world.

I used to go to the expensive coffee shop downtown but it got weird. There were always homeless guys loitering around out front, and I felt like an asshole when I walked past and didn't have change for them, meanwhile I'm carrying a venti frapacrapa with whipped cream that cost more than a down payment on a car.

See what some other Idiots had to say about coffee shops.

"I am really an actor/screenplay writer. That is where I am most proficient. I usually dress up really artsy like and go into a coffee shop with my laptop. All black. Turtle necks in mid-July. Fake glasses. And I never shave my neck. It makes me feel like I am getting things accomplished." ~ Edison – a wannabe bohemian.

"Drinking coffee perks me up and makes me feel more creative. That is how I created a lot of inventions. None of which panned out, but if they do...hello million dollars." ~ Fred – inspiring inventor.

"I never heard of it being against coffee shop policy to not wear a shirt while sitting at a table. That rule is a little strange in my opinion." ~ Chuck – New Hartford, NY.

"There's that damned homeless guy again. Doesn't he have anything else to do? Maybe if I grab the free apartment guide I can pretend to read it while I walk by him." ~ Thom – Columbia, SC.

VII

Traveling Idiots

Airports

Fact: There are 61k people in the air over on any day in the U.S. Idiot Fact: Most of the 61k don't have a clue when they travel.

Idiots must love to travel, because airports are always full of them. You just know from the moment you book your ticket that you are in for an odd experience. I usually stroll into the airport dodging idiots left and right who act like they have never wheeled luggage around before. It's not like they are driving a U-Haul around with a huge trailer. It's a bag with a couple of wheels. I am still not so sure how people lose complete control of them and start weaving all over the place. Good thing they aren't flying the plane.

My main goal as I enter the airport is to try to avoid any conversation with the airline workers. I prefer to carry my luggage on the plane and if your eyes connect with the eyes of an airline worker, you might as well just check your bag. It all of a sudden becomes an intense investigation into your bags' intentions. They start questioning your bag size, contents, age, height, width, weight, religious beliefs and marital status. I wasn't even aware luggage could wed, but then again, times are changing.

Once you pass the counters and kiosks, it's off to the security line, where most of the security guards seem less equipped to keep us safe, than their empty chair with a jacket draped over it. The least they could do is tuck in their shirt and put the oversized slushy cups where we can't see them. Humor us would ya? Security guards, or as we would call them in the grocery store "cashiers," are our first line of defense. I think a cashier would do a better job at keeping us safe. At least a cashier would let me keep my water after scanning it.

This is where you see Idiots start popping up all over the place. By now, most people know the rules when going through the line. The first thing you learn is that you can't wear shoes of any kind, can't wear metal and need to put electronic devices in a separate bin on the conveyor belt. Why is it that people still refuse to take off their shoes, wear metal through the metal detector, leave laptops in their bags and try to get through with big bottles of water? I mean, none of these preventative measures are going to matter anyway, but you shouldn't be holding up the line, because you think you can get away with it.

Idiots will just keep going through a metal detector taking off one item at a time, only to realize it is the last piece of metal they are wearing. Really... what did you think your belt clasp was made out of? Plastic? Boots count as shoes and water is a type of liquid. I am sure one idiot is wondering if he freezes the water, if that would be okay...

After you finally make it through the lines, you are on your way to find a seat to wait for your flight. Hopefully you can find a seat to sit down in and not have to worry about some Idiot with four bags taking them up. Does your bag really need to sit in a chair and wait for your flight? Are we to assume that your bag is too exhausted to stand up on its own and needs a chair? Some people think it is easier to just leave their bags and head to get some food. This move also marks their territory so they have a seat when they return. There are signs posted everywhere that say: "If you see something, say something." I would be saying something constantly. I see a bag on a chair that some Idiot left there. I see another moron who is sprawled out with his feet in the isle so I can't get by. He also left his bag of food lying on the floor.

What's up with the food at airports anyway? It is as if the airport owners went out and did some food tastings to find the worst tasting food in America. Why does it seem acceptable to have crappy food at airports? Have you ever felt confident about getting something decent to eat there? And sometimes, just sometimes they will have a chain restaurant to sit down at, like Outback. Who wants to get to the airport with enough time to sit down and enjoy a meal? So let's review the choices. Get to the airport at a reasonable time and eat crap, or get there really early to sit down and enjoy a more expensive crappy meal. Both options sound excellent.

The best food I ever saw someone eat at an airport was a full size cantaloupe. Who brings a full size cantaloupe to an airport and eats it with a plastic knife? It's not like it's a snickers bar that slips into your pocket. We are talking about a beach ball sized fruit full of seeds and stringy things that has to be carried in while you schlep your luggage. Who does that you ask?

Have you ever had a flight delayed or canceled? I have over heard many Idiots outraged at flight cancellations as if they would prefer risking a plane crash in a storm over a 1 hour delay. Those same people storm up to the airport staff and yell at them as if it was their decision. Talk about problems of a first world country. Boo-hoo, my flight from New York to LA was delayed 30 minutes. It used to be a 6 month journey by boat with half the people dying of scurvy along the way.

"I need to get to Albuquerque. What the hell! Just because it is sleeting, lightening and no visibility don't matter. I have to have my affair." ~ Oswald - a Tuna enthusiast

Hotels

Fact: The life of a typical hotel pillow is 18 to 36 months.
Idiot Fact: People do all sorts of things to the pillows in 18 to 36 months.

Traveling can be an enjoyable experience and a big part of that is the hotel you stay in. When staying in a hotel, you will notice that they are trying hard to compete for your business. Some of them offer you cheap rates, free breakfast, color TV's in your room, an apple or cookie upon check-in, trying to win you over. The fact that I mentioned color TV's was supposed to be funny. Of course they have color TV's!

But is it enough?

When I check into hotels, I never remember thinking, "You know what would make this check-in perfect? A nice hard green apple!" I'm on vacation, not on the Biggest Loser. For some reason hotels try gimmicks like this, hoping that it will make you feel important. Instead of handing me some produce, they should concentrate on shortening the check-in lines. You would think that you're waiting in line to see Justin Bieber, with how long they are. That is of course if you like that sort of thing, which I definitely don't, so let's change the subject.

After I wait for what seems like three days, I am asked to hand over my credit card. Ah yes, this is how the hotel has total control over you. So, you need my card for incidentals? Incidentals is a word that basically means, "Anything we feel like charging you. " I am thinking in the back of my mind that they will charge a bunch of stuff to my room and there is nothing I can do about it. At this point, I am almost done checking in. I start getting that feeling again. You know, when you can start to feel a creepy bell hop guy staring at you wanting to take your bags?

Let me rephrase that, he doesn't want to take your bags, he just wants a tip. As hard as it sounds to roll a 20lb bag around, I think I can do it. It doesn't do me any good to hand a stranger my personal belongings, only to have to wait in the room until they bring them.

I don't want him bringing my bags, as it is, now he is going to enter my bedroom with them and I have to wait an extra 10 minutes? What if I have to go to the bathroom when I get to the room? Should I or shouldn't I go? Will the bell hop knock when I am sitting on the can? Of course they always take longer than expected and they are as unpredictable as jungle cats. They are probably going through my bag as they roll it. A pleasant thought indeed. Next time I will load up my bags with bear traps to see what happens.

Anyway, as soon as I find my room after walking through a maze, I have no confidence that the key card will work. For me at least, they never work. After the 3rd try, the green light goes on and I am in. I feel like I am in the movie Mission Impossible and I have just cracked the code. The first thing I see are bottles of $7 spring water. You know the kind of $7 spring water that would go great after eating an awful hard apple. Then I think to myself, should I just drink it? They are probably going to charge it to my card anyway for incidentals. Just as I decide not to drink it, I hear a pounding at the door. It's the creepy bell hop looking for his $5 tip that he is going to force me to give him. I usually give $2, but I said $5, because I didn't want to sound cheap to the people reading this book. Not only do I prefer carrying my own stuff, I now have to pay the guy for most likely rummaging through it and for wasting my time. After I pay the man, it is time to inspect the room.

There are no bed bugs in the bed, which is ridiculous that we have to look now-a-days. I might as well check the closet for the boogie man, because I always thought bed bugs weren't real either.

I think the most important thing is to make sure that the toilet paper in the bathroom is folded into a triangle, because that really classes up the joint. If you think about it, the last person in there ripped off a piece and wiped their rump. Mr. Poopy hands could have touched that nice looking triangle before it was folded up. I just figured you should know about Mr. Poopy hands.

"My favorite part of the toilet paper is the triangle." ~ Mr. Poopy hands of Selkirk NY.

Moving on in your room, you can almost guarantee that your pillows are going to be the most uncomfortable pillows you have ever slept on. Who has those big fluffy pillows at their home anyway? You know the ones you put your head in and it immediately collapses around your face making it hard to breathe or scream for help? That will be good for waking you up 7 or 8 times during the night with screeching neck pain and gasping for air. You won't even need your alarm clock either, because you will already be up from the pillows.

And who trusts the alarm clocks in hotels? Most of the time it takes a genius to figure out how to set them. I usually look at it for about a minute and then call down to the receptionist to make sure she wakes me up in the morning. I put all my trust in the people who gave me my apple when I checked-in. "I have an important meeting, can you please call me at 5 am and make sure I am up? I am assuming that you are going to be working 14 hours straight. Thanks!" If I am lucky to wake up on time, I consider it a victory.

When I am at a hotel, I all of a sudden feel lazy and wasteful. I probably use four or five towels to dry off in the morning and use the rest to step on in the bathroom. I have the air conditioning at about 45 degrees, leave the TV on all night, leave the bathroom light on, but close the door so the light doesn't bother me and have the hotel staff ready to wake me up in the morning for the free breakfast they are about to cook for me. Yup, I'm taking some advantage. I put the AC on full blast and pull up extra comforters.

VIII

Idiots and Their Health

Fact: You burn more calories sleeping than you do watching TV. Idiot Fact: Some people consider sleeping working out.

In 2013, nothing is more important than one's health. Actually, this has pretty much been the most important thing throughout history. But it's a lot more trendy now. With gym memberships on the rise, yoga, Pilates, cross training, Zumba, and fad diets everywhere, people want to look and feel good. All right, let's get real, people just want to look good. If we could choose a perfect body accompanied by a heart attack at age 60 or five-hundred excess pounds but live to 110, I think we all know what most people would prefer.

Routine checkups at the doctor's office are very important for preventative measures. But there are plenty of reasons people avoid the doctor's office, myself included. I mean, if I don't know anything is wrong then I don't have to worry about it. And if preventative health measures are so important like everyone says, why the hell is the medical system so difficult?

Recently, I made an appointment with the doctor. Of course I couldn't call from work because as soon as I start talking everyone within ear shot clams up and starts eavesdropping. Strangers are delivering unnecessary papers to my desk. Someone is hiding behind a nearby plant. Another is wearing a fake mustache and glasses holding a Styrofoam cup up to his ear. They hear the dreaded phrase "blood work" and instantly think I have a disease and they need to avoid me (which most of the time is fine by me.)

Despite work taking money out of my check for health insurance, I still had to pay for the cryptic copay. I'm with the doctor for sixty seconds. He looks at me and says "Yes I can see you…schedule an appointment." Then he turned me over to the receptionist.

I thought this was an appointment?

Now I have to go and schedule another session with his majesty. More time off from work a week from now, and guess what? Another copay. What's worse is a few weeks later, I get a bill in the mail for something that isn't covered by the insurance. The doctor took my blood pressure and that device isn't covered by your plan, don't you know? And they wonder why people don't go to the doctor. And then the "This is not a bill" letter comes in the mail. Of course they make absolutely no sense. No one can translate them. If this isn't a bill, stop scaring me with your guesstimates of what I have to pay. One of these days I am going to send them a fake check and say this isn't your payment.

So a few days and a thinner wallet later, I go back for my new appointment. I'm sitting in the waiting room which is probably the most uncomfortable place on the planet, including Antarctica. I'm surrounded by the downtrodden. They are all sicker than me, I've convinced myself. What to do to pass the time? On the coffee table, which is misleading because there is no coffee anywhere, sits countless magazines that sick people flip through after blowing their noses. And none of the reading material is ever decent either. I could read last month's Sports Illustrated, but since the cover is a preview of the NFL Playoffs and the Super Bowl has been over for almost a month, I decide to people watch again.

There's that nurse again. She's just walking around clutching a folder. She goes to the front desk and chats with the receptionist. Then she walks around with the folder some more. What's in the folder? Is it the equivalent of a football in a game of...football? Will the other staff tackle her?

"Screw that! I use Web MD. And I'm pretty darn good at diagnosing myself. Last week I took orange juice to beat a case of scarlet fever." ~ Clyde – a man who watches reruns of ER.

"These doctors don't belong giving advice. I only watch and respect Doctor Oz." ~ Maryanne – Bridgewater, MN.

"My pregnant wife was in for a checkup and the fat nurse was telling her it's okay to follow her cravings. Eat a greasy cheeseburger she says! Pile on the bacon! It's great for the baby! Judging by her waistline, she ought to avoid giving healthy eating advice." ~ Frank – proud father.

I continue to wait. As I look around the office, I see a bunch of advertisements for various drugs I could take. I am sure the side effect jokes are already played out, but let's do one more for the hell of it. Do your toe nails grow too fast?

Sick of clipping them? Take Toeziack Plus. In a recent study, Toeziack Plus saw a 12% reduction in toenail growth in patients who don't like fast growing toenails. Side effects include; loss of appetite, continual vomiting, hearing loss, sudden death, kidney malfunction, skin loss, weight gain, severe weight loss, man boobs, insomnia, bad breath, shortness of breath, loss of toes, increased armpit hair growth, and in some cases increased speed of toenail growth.

Dentist

**Fact: You should replace your toothbrush every three months.
Idiot Fact: People without teeth might not need to.**

As bad as the doctor's office is, the dentist could be even worse. I just had an appointment to get my teeth cleaned and since I'd had the appointment scheduled for six months, I figured I better not miss it. I try to time my eating of candy to a few weeks before so if I do get a cavity my teeth won't fall out waiting for the next available time slot to open up. And how funny is it that I go years without seeing a doctor for a physical, but never miss a dentist appointment? Basically I'm saying who cares if my insides are garbage, as long as I have a nice smile.

Of course I brush and floss right before going in, sort of like cramming for an exam. Like if I hadn't been brushing my teeth every day the dentist would be fooled by me doing it one time just before the appointment. That's like someone overweight doing a sit-up before going to see a trainer.

I sign in at the desk and the girl asks if I want the fluoride treatment. Of course…why wouldn't I? As I make a mental note to Google what the hell the fluoride treatment is when I get home. And of course, the girl working there takes me to get my teeth x-rayed and wants to chat. There's no way of talking as she's stuffing a piece of cardboard between my gums and teeth. Then she puts a 4-inch thick vest over my torso that looks like it could absorb a bullet. Hooray! My chest is safe! My face? Not so much, as she puts the x-ray machine half an inch from my jaw and starts blasting a series of pictures. I can't wait to see the effects of that in 20 years.

Finally I'm in the chair waiting. I glance around at all the posters advertising teeth whitening. Apparently I'll not only get a better smile if I do this, but I'll have perfect hair, skin, and a trophy wife. And why is it that the dental hygienist who makes far less than the dentist a year is the one who does all the work? (including trying to have an actual conversation while my mouth is full of instruments.) Meanwhile, the dentist who makes 300k a year comes in for 30 seconds, pokes randomly at one tooth and leaves, of course after reminding me I'm not flossing enough. I could floss 25 times a day and they will still make a dig at me like I don't know what floss is. Then continue to make me feel guilty and bad about myself. There isn't much else that could make you feel guiltier than not flossing.

And after the cleaning is done, why does she ask if I want to rinse? No thanks, I prefer the taste of blood, metal, cotton and chalk in my mouth.

Oh, I forgot to mention I am wearing a bib like a 2 year old, that she has to take off for me, because apparently I can't figure out how. Finally I'm done. They hand me a miniature tube of toothpaste and a cheap brush that looks like it was stolen from a hotel.

Now that I am humiliated by the Dentist, it's off to the receptionist I go. My insurance covers everything, except for the fluoride treatment of course, and they'll send me a bill for three dollars. She goes to schedule my next appointment and asks if I'm free November 5th (today is May 1st). Um…sure…I guess…seriously?

"I like getting the bubblegum flavored toothpaste at the dentist. It makes me really happy. Cavities don't make me happy though." ~ Sven – 47 year old man from PA

Smoking

Fact: About 19% of people smoke.
Idiot Fact: Most of them still think it makes them look cool.

One thing it doesn't take a medical school diploma to understand is the unhealthiest thing to do is smoke. Haven't we figured out that smoking isn't good for you? And at $10 a pack, come on.

I love how people on TV shows and commercials used to smoke back in the 50's and 60's when they "didn't know it was bad for you." Right. Like lighting a piece of paper on fire, sticking it in your mouth and inhaling could ever possibly be good for you. Generally the first thing that happens when you smoke is you cough, which is your lungs way of indicating that what you are doing is not too bright and you should probably stop.

Smokers can be Idiots for a lot of reasons other than what they do to themselves. Like why do they throw cigarette butts in the street or out the window of their cars? Do they think the people behind them enjoy a sparking object flying at their car? They act like it's not the same as littering. And I love it when they stick a piece of gum in their mouth after they finish a cigarette, like they could possible cover up that filthy smell. And the smokers at work drive me insane. They think they are entitled to 10 times as many breaks as the rest of us. I once heard a coworker who smokes say she couldn't get through a stressful situation without a smoke break. If I said the same thing except substituted smoke break for a highball of vodka, they'd say I have a problem.

And why is it that smokers are always asking me for a lighter?

"Smoking is cool, end of story." Cough...wheeze... ~ Gary – a smoker.

"I don't carry no lighter on me dog. I just roll up on some fool or some hot shorty and it's like, you got a lighter dog?" ~ BJ – A smoker who doesn't carry a lighter.

Gym

Fact: The average monthly gym membership is $55.
Idiot Fact: Some people put on makeup before they go to the gym.

So how does one get healthier? How about joining a gym? Ah yes the gym…some come to socialize, some to meet their significant other. One or two actually go to work out. Most have no reason to go at all, but they do anyway.

There are so many Idiots at the gym to choose from.

There's the guy who is just there to pick up girls and doesn't exercise at all – and if you watch him closely, he never gets any girls either. That's what we call a double waste of time and money. There's the guy who wants to work in with you, apparently he doesn't see the 5,000 other pieces of equipment and just has to do what you are doing right then and there. Or the guy that comes up when you're in the middle of something and asks if you're done with that. Does it look like I'm finished Captain Idiot? There's always a guy who's occupying 5 different machines at once with a conveniently placed water bottle sitting on a flat bench while he's 50 feet away working on the fly machine or talking to some other Idiot. You sit down and do a set or two, he comes over to inform you that "he's on that machine" really? If you were, then I wouldn't be sitting here now.

I like the guy who has no organized routine; he's just randomly doing a couple reps on every machine. "Here's my workout; three dumbbell curls, five crunches, and two squats." Then there's the guy who is lifting way too much weight for his strength. He can curl 50 pounds by flailing his back and tossing his entire body weight into the movements, while making animal sounds. Good job buddy, not only did you not impress anyone with your lack of strength, you slipped three discs and got the beginnings of a hernia started.

Ever been to the gym on a weekday morning when you usually go in the evening? It's a whole different world with completely different people. They usually look at you like you're the new guy and you've invaded their turf. Sometimes I go during the day if I'm not working and see someone that I usually see at night. Either this guy has the same day off as me or he lives here.

The new thing everyone is talking about is cross training. And when I say talking, I mean blabbering a lot about it. The concept is this. You still work out, but instead of the old boring repetition style lifting, you do more functional and core exercises. Instead of using normal looking weights and dumbbells, you use tires, ropes and other stuff that make you look like a dumbbell. Not only do these exercises make you look foolish, they are called ridiculous things too. Today's work out is 15 crappies, 30 bumpkins, 50 dungs-ups and 32 yuckels. When you are done with that, you have to run down a rocky hill with a shopping cart over your head. What? This will get me in shape? It will probably also get me on YouTube with a video titled "Look at this Idiot!"

You know it is the new craze, because people have to insist on telling you about what they did the night before, what they are going to do and of course how great of a work out they got. I've seen heavy people do these exercises, gloat about how great it is and never change physically.

"Do you want me to tell you about my work out? Probably not, but I am going to go ahead and tell you anyway. And, if you aren't fortunate enough for me to tell you in person, I will post on Facebook about it. Gotta make sure everyone knows what I am doing. " ~ Everyone who does these workouts.

"Why do fat people always walk side by side so no one can get around them?" ~ Sal – Jock at the gym with Italian flag tattoo on his shoulder.

And they also have you on weird diets. Suddenly it is okay to eat things high in fat. Go ahead, eat a pack of bacon. Drink heavy crème instead of milk. Substitute vegetable oil instead of drinking water. Did they just gather up foods that no other diet is using? Let's see here, Mediterranean Diet has Olive oil. Atkins has protein. South Beach is dumb and without plastic surgery you won't look like people from Miami anyway. Well, I guess the only items that haven't been claimed are sugar and fat. Let's go with fat. I saw a guy cook a plate of bacon at work and think it was okay because he is cross training. Really? Are we supposed to believe that drinking heavy cream isn't bad for you? Come on.

You always hear how short their workouts are too. "All you need is a tractor tire and 3 minutes a day." You just have to work out really hard though during that time.

"Ate five hotdogs yesterday. It's okay though. I pushed a tire around. Besides it's the good fat." ~ Charlie F. Cross Train extraordinaire.

"Did a bunch of Crappies and feel great. Gonna lay on the floor next and have someone drive a car over my abs. It is supposedly a core workout for my chest." ~ A loser

And of course every gym has a grunter. This is the huge guy benching a silly amount of weight screaming and grunting. He usually has several tribal armband tattoos and gallon jug of oddly colored liquid. We get it, you're strong.

"I like to take a drink of water after everything I do. You would think I was in a dessert." - Miles – a procrastinating weight lifter.

The clothing choices some people have at the gym make me wonder, what the hell are people thinking? For starters…men and tank tops. Just don't do it. I have no interest in seeing your hairy armpits or the Italian flag you have tattooed on your shoulder. And I really hate using a machine after you've sweat all over it. You aren't restricted by a tee-shirt. It's almost as silly as the big muscle-man benching in a hoodie. Chances are, you don't have as good of a body as you think you do.

"Sup…my workout clothes are very important to me. They speak volumes about my style at the gym. Hair be all spiked and gelled up good, tank top be showing my bod. I got soccer sneakers on, and bike pants. People are intimidated. They know I pretty much call the shots at the gym." ~ Burt– A typical gym rat.

"If I don't look good, I don't feel good. If that's the case, I must be feeling pretty good right…right? What the hell are you looking at? Me, that's who. ~ Chase – Employee of his father's pizza shop.

"The chicks man, it's all about the chicks. I work hard mentally at the office. I go to the gym to give my body just as hard a workout. The chicks come here for a show and no other reason, so I'm here to give them that show. Every day that I can. We expect the chicks to look good, so we need to look good for the chicks. It's a two way street. Or a three-way if you get lucky with two chicks." ~ Pete – a thirty-something grown man that still refers to women as chicks.

A few guys at my gym work out in jeans. Strange choice, but I'll take that any day over the old naked men in the locker room. I mean come on, put on a towel. They stand there stark naked having conversations like it's completely acceptable that their wrinkled old bodies and genitals are flailing about.

I also think there should be an age limit to even enter the gym. Let's say, minimum age thirty. This may make me sound old, but I hate kids running around. Nothing is worse than when I set my sights on doing a particular machine and there is some pimple faced teenager sitting on it barely using any weight. Dude, just leave. Don't you have some reefer to smoke?

Some people say the gym is a great place to meet women. Not really the case nowadays. Every girl has earphones on or their running at full speed on a treadmill. There is no way to talk to that. And besides, there's always a stronger guy walking around.

My favorite gym girl is the one in the skin tight trashy outfit, the word 'Pink' or 'Hottie' splashed across her buttocks with her hair and nails done, as well as wearing makeup. She can usually be found sitting on an exercise bike pedaling so slowly as to not break a sweat and reading a magazine. Seriously, if you can read while working out, you're not working out.

And why am I the only person that can just work out in silence. It's not 90 minutes of the "Dave" show with screaming and grunting and futile cries for attention.

This one guy stops working out to take a call. He's walking around on his cell phone talking to god knows who about how he is going to beat some kid up at a party. Seriously you're an Idiot.

I think we can all agree that the worst time to have a gym membership is January. I have to park 50 miles away the month of January because of Idiots and New Year's resolutions to exercise. At least I think the resolution was to exercise, even though I just see extra cars in the parking lot and people standing around chatting inside.

"My resolution is to get in shape! I go to the gym every Monday and Thursday, and each morning have bowl of Cocoa Krispies." ~ Darrel - someone who doesn't really want to get in shape.

Speaking of losing weight, why is it that overweight people always get to celebrate when they lose weight? What about some claps for me? I have always stayed in shape. Shouldn't I be the one who gets the recognition? Do I have to put on some pounds and then take it off to get a little respect?

VIII

Holidays, weddings, and funerals, oh my...

**Fact: 10 Million U.S. consumers wait until the day of, to buy a gift.
Idiot Fact: Most people don't like the gifts you buy.**

Wedding bells are in the air. Can you hear them? Maybe it's just the sound of your eardrums begging you to RSVP, no thank you. The sound of wedding bells sounds an awful lot like the sound of your bank account moving in the downward direction. Do you like that sound? No? We didn't think you did. But do you ever say anything about it? Probably not. Cha-ching!

Weddings are sometimes a lot of fun, but can sometimes be a big pain in the ass. They didn't used to be though. Back in the day, everyone lived close to one another, so travel was basically nonexistent. You could swing down to the local wedding hall and have a nice inexpensive wedding and a good time. That changed however when people realized they could fall in love with someone out of their zip code. What Idiots!

It all starts the moment someone gets engaged and jots down your name as someone they want at their wedding. At this point, they aren't really thinking about the amount of money you will have to spend to travel, eat, lodge and bring a gift for them. All of a sudden, that celebration turns into your new unexpected bill. It's not just the wedding either, it is everything else that goes with it. The prequel if you will.

From dinners and drinks, to the celebration of a ring sliding on a finger, to bachelor parties in different countries and weddings that require passports with no nonstop flights. Yes, someone is clearly only thinking about themselves.

It all started with some stuck up, spoiled little princess back in the day. She had been dreaming about her wedding since she was eight and her daddy, gladly forked over the cash for whatever she wanted. A photographer for $25,000? Sure. Flowers that cost $8,000? No problem honey, do whatever you want. Because of this, every wedding facility knows they can get away with charging an arm and a leg. After all, it is your special day. It's simple economics. If we all agreed to get married for one-hundred bucks, that's all they could charge. But we can't. And it's all thanks to that stupid little princess.

The expenses start the moment someone gets engaged. "Let's go out to eat at an expensive restaurant to celebrate!" Single friends probably aren't that excited and chances are that they think you made a big mistake. That's some great reassurance, isn't it? Especially for the single friends. They would like nothing more than for you to be single so it takes the pressure off of them. On the other hand, your married friends aren't really excited, because they already got married and went through the process. They have already decided that their special day is going to be better than yours and it isn't going to compare, no matter what you do. You could have a dinosaur carry the flowers down the aisle and they will be like...been there, done that.

So as you prepare for your wedding, what can you do to save face? Try this. Make the wedding inexpensive for your guests. People don't usually have more fun with the more you spend. We don't want to go to a fancy hotel if it means we have to pay fancy hotel prices. $1,200 a night is a little overboard. Number two, having the wedding across the country is not making it appealing to people on the East Coast. So if you met all of your friends on the East Coast, have the wedding on the East Coast. Number Three, do you really need 9 groomsman? Because 8 of them don't want to be in the wedding or spend the money.

But really... we hope you have the best first wedding of your life. Since 60% of marriages end in divorce, it's a safe bet to keep notes on what worked and what didn't, so you're better prepared for the inevitable next time.

"My wedding is very special and I don't care how much my friends have to spend." ~ Luther - professional skee-ball arcade game player.

Did you ever try talking to the Groom or Bride during a wedding or reception? How awkward can that be? It's like you don't even know them and you are talking to them for the first time.

Sample Conversation:
Guest: How's it going?
Groom: It's going.
What in the hell does that mean?
Guest: Have a great wedding day!

Really? Is there a time limit on how long something great can be? Should I only enjoy today and not my honeymoon? I think it would be better to say, "Have a great life." Or at least "Have a great month." On the other hand, if you say have a great life, people tend to get offended. Maybe I should just stick to a time limit after all!

And why do people say *"with my luck"* always assuming something bad will happen. Everyone says that, so does everyone have bad luck? *"With my luck, it will rain on my wedding day."* Did you ever hear someone say: *"With my luck, it will be a beautiful day."* Try it sometime and I guarantee people will think you are nuts.

"With my luck it will rain on my wedding day and Henry will leave me at the altar." ~ Trisha - Norfolk Virginia.

Holidays

Fact: The #1 gift that gets returned during the holidays is clothes.
Idiot Fact: Holidays are stressful. Don't make them more stressful.

Idiots like to come out in clusters around the holidays. It starts the day after Halloween when they start putting giant inflatable snowmen in the yards despite it still being 60 degrees out. At Thanksgiving we deal with Idiots wearing pilgrim and turkey hats, saying things like, "Happy Turkey Day!" Like it's too tough to say Thanksgiving.
And of course the day before everyone has to remind me not to eat too much turkey. Thanks, I had planned on eating four full turkeys. Good thing I ran into you first.

Christmas is great too, or as some in the now PC world prefer to call it, a winter celebration. I don't know about you but I don't celebrate sub-zero temperatures and dirty slush all over the roads, during winter. Christmas commercials are great too. I like the one where the guy surprises his wife with a brand new shiny Lexus (complete with a bow) like that isn't the kind of thing you would discuss first with your wife before buying. And did you shop at Tiffany's for a necklace? Have you seen the prices there? No, I did not.

And I'm no zoological expert, but I'm pretty sure polar bears wouldn't want to drink soda. Nothing says Christmas like a nice healthy serving of GMO high fructose corn syrup.

Elf on the Shelf has become really popular. It is essentially a story about some guy in tights, that hides around your house spying on your kids. No wonder I can't get my daughter to go to sleep. "Hey honey, sleep tight and be good because a weird man in tights will be peaking at you when you sleep. Have a good sleep!"

"I put Elf on the Shelf in many different poses. My 3 month old loves it. Then I take 200 pictures of the Elf and post them on Facebook so all of my friends can see. They love it." ~ Someone who doesn't realize they post far too many pictures of crap on Facebook.

Baby & Wedding Showers

Fact: Most have one baby shower, even if they have more kids.
Idiot Fact: It's better to not get drunk and act foolish at a shower.

Baby showers can be a very uncomfortable experience. The people having them might as well send out an invitation that says, "Buy me a bunch of crap, so I don't have to. But, don't buy any old crap. I don't want you to try and think outside of the box, because I probably won't like what you are going to get."

That is where registry's come into play. They are created to make life easier for the people buying gifts. The logic is simple really. You look at the list, buy something, and you are done. You know the person will like it, because they asked for it. Deep down we all know that people would prefer cash, but items on the registry will suffice. With that said, I can't figure out why people end up getting items that are not on the registry or don't just give cash.

Gee, thanks for the waffle blender! It will look great in my basement stuffed behind the 7 coolers I've collected. We understand you have an imagination. Great! We just prefer you don't use it.

Opening the gifts can be a really awkward time for the parents and for the guests who gave them. First off for the parents, it is very hard to fake liking things you don't. I'm not going to beat a dead horse here, but that goes back to following the list of items people ask for on their registry.

Smiling and saying that a spatula is great and acting excited can be downright exhausting. "Oh boy a wooden spoon, thank you so so much. I'm going to use this to stir things." Really? No shit! And why do we find it necessary to say what the gift is as we're opening it, as though all other people in the room are blind. "It's a blender!" Yeah, we can see that. "Joey has been saying he wants to blend things lately. Thank you." There's also no need to add further comments on when you will use the gift. "We have a BBQ coming up (that none of you are invited to). We can blend ice with it then." Just be quiet. Classic over compensation.

I've been on the other side of the coin too. I've bought gifts and had to sit there and watch people open them. I mean, if you purchase something on the list... well you know, they have to like it and you are all set right? Not exactly. There is always the fear of seeming too cheap. What if the person's presents that are opened before mine are super expensive? What if they bought them a house? Will the pacifiers I bought look too insignificant? Sometimes you have to add in some commentary to make your present look better. "Oh, those pacifiers? Yeah, Brad Pitt gives the same kind to his kids and Brad Pitt is super rich and famous. I had to drive an extra mile to get my hands on those. Spent a little extra in gas and wasted 3 more minutes of my day, but it was nothing really. That is what I do for such good friends like you."

"I saw Samantha's registry, but I really think she is going to be super excited for the gift I decided to get her instead. A ship in a bottle sandwich maker! How unique is that! She is going to love it. It is way better than cash or anything on her dumb registry." ~ Monica aka terrible gift giver – Jonestown Missouri

Birthdays

Fact: Birthdays happen once a year.
Idiot Fact: Taking a shot for every year of your age is not smart.

Do we ever get to an age where you can tone down birthdays? As an adult, am I still expected to buy streamers and balloons for another adult? Do I need to hire a clown too? What about the people who design birthday cards? First off, just having to buy them is Idiotic and annoying. No one cares if you are one year older. If you're over the age of 10, you don't need a birthday card. The process is draining to say the least. I have to go to the store, pick one out, then of course I don't have any stamps because no one mails things anymore, (except stupid cards) so now I have to go buy a stamp... I think you get what I am saying.

The real problem with birthday cards is I only have two choices. Extremely sappy or extremely stupid. Picture this, so it's my dad's birthday and I need to get him a card because he likes it and my mom will yell at me if I don't. He is a 75 year old full blooded Italian and former U.S. Air Force pilot. My birthday card options: A picture of purple flowers peacefully sitting in a sun filled meadow and the caption – "To my loving father," complete with a poem by W.B. Yeats, or a cartoonish photo of an obese slob sitting on a toilet and some wisecrack about chili and hemorrhoids.

Um...no thanks.

I keep looking. I manage to find one that's not offensive or stupid, but the other birthday card problem arises: they are insanely specific. The card itself is perfect, but it's of course from "the three of us" which isn't applicable to me (unless I count the voices in my head). I find another good one but it's addressed to my adoptive father. Maybe I can just cross that part out. Here's another great one...oh wait...it's a happy birthday from the family dog. Damn it!

At this point I've been in the card section of the store for 45 minutes, trying to select a piece of dead tree that will be in a trash can 96 hours from now anyway.

"I like getting really sappy cards from someone who doesn't have the courage to say it to my face. It is really nice and I feel blessed." ~ Judy, candy enthusiast from Queens NY.

Funerals

Fact: Everyone dies in their lifetime.
Idiot Fact: We had to look that one up too.

Is there anything worse than dying? Some people say life is too short, but really, it's the longest thing there is. So, close your eyes and think of the most awkward time of your life. Got it? Ok, now take that place and put a corpse in a box in the middle of the room. Are you with me so far? Great. Now, start talking to some people that you don't fully know while they are crying. How is it going so far? Good?
After talking to those people you barely know, while they are crying, make your way up to the dead guy and get down on your knees in front of him. No pressure at all, but you are supposed to be saying a prayer that you don't really have memorized. Bits and pieces of it should suffice right? Just mutter a couple of words, a couple Amens and you should be good. Don't wait too long, because another awkward individual is waiting right behind you to do the same thing.

Are you supposed to smile at all? I don't know what to say to people who lose their favorite CD let alone their favorite family member. That my friend is your new most awkward time of your life.

It's a nice culture we have, who came up with the idea of standing around socializing in a room with a corpse. No wonder we love zombie movies so much. And why do I feel awkward? I'm 6 inches from a body and then have to shake hands and hug a row of sobbing people, most of whom I don't know. Why am I the one that feels like a fool? No one here cares about me, yet I feel awkward. The luckiest person in the room is the guy in the box. He has the least amount of responsibilities.

"I enjoy going to funerals and crying with people. They don't know who I am most of the time, but it makes me feel like I accomplished something." ~ Sid – Gas pump cleaner

X

Idiots and sports go hand in hand...

Fact: Chances are you won't make a professional sports team. Idiot Fact: Most people act like their softball beer league is as competitive as the pros.

Or hand in glove, if you will. You see, Idiots follow sports. Idiots play sports. Idiots report on sports. Networks devote 24 hour coverage of Idiots just lecturing about sports.

Let's cover some ground rules.

Never say "we" when talking about a team, unless you are Derek Jeter. There is no need to say "we played poorly last night" or "we are going all the way this year!" We are not doing anything, they are. You are just an Idiot who bought a hat.

Try to remember...when you're playing a beer league softball game...it's not the World Series. You don't need eye black to catch a ball the size of a grapefruit at eight o'clock at night. You also don't need a custom uniform. Cargo shorts and flip-flops will do. And please, don't yell at anyone on your team. Get over yourself, its softball and it's supposed to be fun. The goal of playing is to win if you can, then go to the bar, eat some wings and drink some beer. There won't be a parade for you if you win. It won't be on ESPN, and chances are people will forget about it a day later.

And how annoying is sports comradery? Only at a stadium or sports bar would some complete stranger just push up next to you (with no understanding of personal space) and just start a conversation.

"Wow, the Mets really need pitching."

Um...okay...do you think I'm the guy who makes the trades?

"Thought Johnson was gonna be a good signing for us. What a bust!"

Oh, you're still talking to me. How should I respond to that? I think I'll just nod my head.

And don't complain about their salaries. You know damn well every time you drive by a group of construction workers on the road you're whining that they get paid to stand around and do nothing. And I bet if someone followed you on a daily basis they would say the same thing. It's not unique to sports.

"These bums make millions and do nothing. Boy I wish I made that much."

Okay, thanks for the update. Go make a team then.

There are also fans that find the need to show off how much they love a team by wearing an inordinate amount of team flare. A Red Sox hat will do. You don't need a hat, a tee shirt under an Ortiz jersey, socks, and a keychain clipped to your belt. I get it, you're a fan of the Red Sox. And no one cares if your father, your grandfather, and your great grandfather are all fans of the Red Sox. What does that mean? You've all been following the same stupid team for a hundred years!

One Idiot shows up to work the day after the Yankees get knocked out of the playoffs and he's wearing his "Got Rings" t-shirt which lists the 27 times the Yankees won the world series. Sorry pal, but you weren't alive for 24 of those years.

And there's always that one idiot who has to go against the standard. The office is located in Philadelphia. Everyone in the bar is an Eagles fan, except the one Idiot in the Cowboys hat. Then he starts pointing to his fingers (where he would have rings if they gave them to fans) and reciting the number of times the Cowboys won a Super Bowl.

My favorite of the bunch is that guy who pretends he is the decider of if you should like a team or not, and if you do, are you a genuine fan. If I want to like a team, who cares? Why do I need a stamp of approval?

"How long have you liked them for?"

"How could you like an out of state team when you live in this area?"

"Do you like them because they are good now?"

"Who was the backup shortstop in 1956?"

It's none of your damn business why I like them and what do you care if I do?

Then you got your group that cares so deeply about a team losing, like the world is ending. They usually don't want you to talk to them because they are so upset that a bunch of guys they never met lost a game and you happen to like them. Boohoo. Get over it. They will start playing again in a few months. Then you can start acting like a complete fool all over again.

There are also fans who collect merchandise like cards. Yes, grown men are collecting pictures of younger men and that doesn't seem weird?

Did you ever see the fan who thinks he has an effect on the game? Like if he takes off his shirt in freezing weather, that it will be a good luck charm. There are a bunch of people in parka's, subzero temperatures, and then the one guy standing there in his t-shirt to ignite a rally. What are these people thinking? They aren't. They are just Idiots.

"I've been to 400 games, wear team gear all of the time and have bumper stickers on my car. I am a bigger fan than you are, because I blow tons of money on crap to prove it." Wally ~ That guy who thinks people care how big of a fan he is. – Chicago, Illinois

Conclusion

One thing is for certain, you'll never look at other people the same way again. Whether it's Midge from the office and her obnoxious perfume, or Jim Bob the mechanic making you feel like less of a man for not knowing what sized wipers your car requires, we like to think we educated you just a little bit on Idiots.

What we want is to make you take a good hard think about yourself, and make sure you're not the ire of someone's scorn. Like that guy who cut you off, only to slam on his brakes and make a turn into a driveway, or that Idiot in the cell phone kiosk asking if I need a knit jacket or protective sleeve for my phone (sorry buddy, I need food, water and shelter, not an expensive wardrobe for my phone).

With the knowledge of this book, you'll be able to recognize and react to the tough situations life throws at you. If you enter a bathroom and you hear a cough, it's just someone's way of saying "Hey...I'm in here!" in case the lock on the stall doesn't work.

Keep this book in a safe place. In fact, buy several more copies. You may need them. Use it as a reference, in case you find yourself slipping. Or hand it out to someone else that's in need (or doesn't know that they are). Like the lady in front of you in the drive thru who just can't seem to decide what kind of donut she wants. Or, the guy at the game wearing the Giants jersey that has his own last name embroidered on the back.

If you find yourself in the supermarket and you decide you don't want the steak, just put it back in the meat cooler, or hand it to a clerk. We don't want you to think it's okay to stuff it behind the Time Magazine at the register.

Take this book and use it as a stocking stuffer - or a birthday present for that guy on your Facebook page who's posting pictures of himself in his bathroom mirror.

Remember, Idiots are everywhere. Make sure you do your best to not become one.

Authors Info

Mike and Matt have been friends since the summer of 1987, when Matt's family moved into the neighborhood and a row of trees and a small metal fence divided their backyards.

Both graduates of New Hartford High School, working together came as second nature as the duo would embark on numerous entrepreneurial and entertainment based ventures. Ventures included everything from organized backyard haunted hayrides every October, to charging neighborhood kids admission to watch them play wiffleball.

Mike and Matt also worked on dozens of satirical skits, short films and currently write for a sarcastic baseball blog.

Matt has written two books; a collection of short stories titled *twelve til dawn*, and a novel *Deadly Crossings*.

Thank You!

A special 'Thank You' to Jenny and Matt for editing and reviewing content for "Idiots Are Everywhere." Also, Thank You to all of the Idiots out there that made this book possible.